The Grand

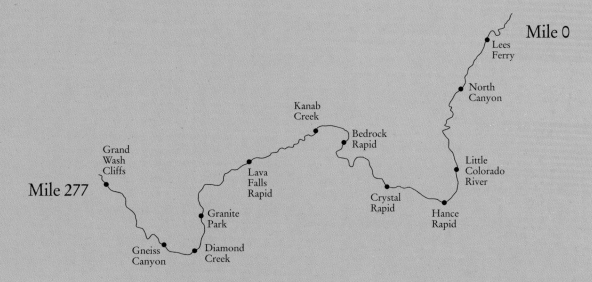

Mile 0

Lees
Ferry

North
Canyon

Little
Colorado
River

Hance
Rapid

Crystal
Rapid

Bedrock
Rapid

Kanab
Creek

Lava
Falls
Rapid

Grand
Wash
Cliffs

Mile 277

Granite
Park

Diamond
Creek

Gneiss
Canyon

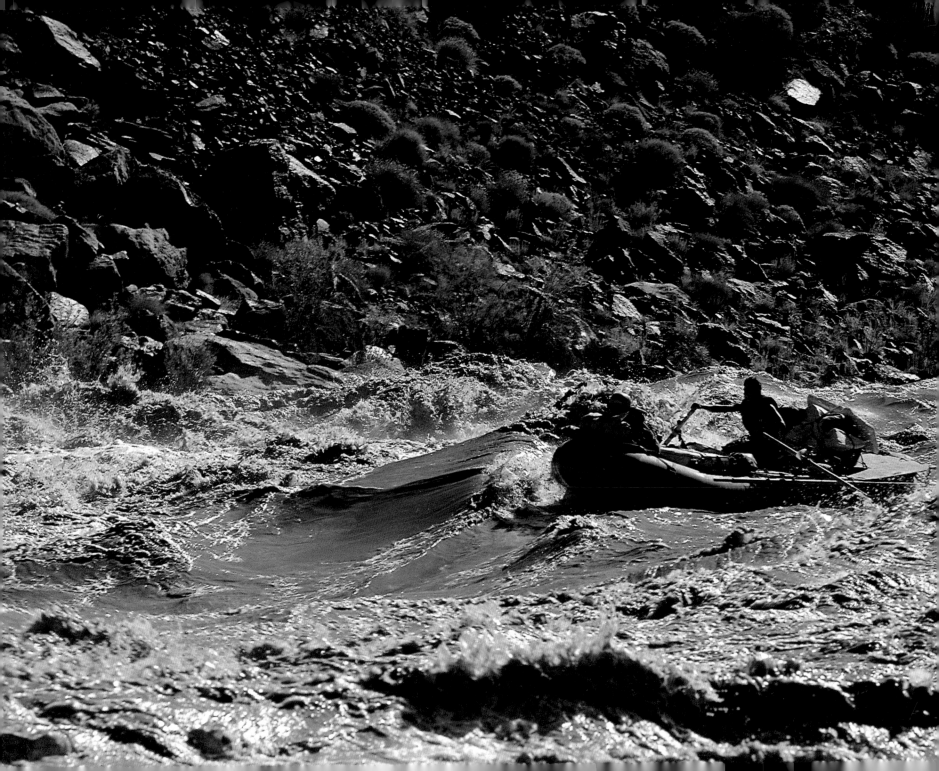

The Grand

The Colorado River
in the Grand Canyon,
a Photo Journey

By Steve Miller

WILDERNESS PRESS

GRAND CANYON
ASSOCIATION

In memory of my father, **Robert Miller**, who first took me to the Grand Canyon, and my stepson, **Brahm Reynolds**, a talented river guide who drowned while kayaking on the South Fork of the Payette River in Idaho.

The Grand: The Colorado River in the Grand Canyon, a Photo Journey
1st EDITION September 2005
Copyright © 2005 by Steve Miller
All photos, except where noted, copyright © 2005 by Steve Miller
Map on pages 4-5 copyright © 2005 by Grand Canyon Association
Graphic of geologic formations on page 188 copyright © 2005 by Grand Canyon Association
Cover and interior design: Jeremy G. Stout
Book editor: Eva Dienel
Library of Congress Card Number 2005047057

ISBN 0-89997-367-1
UPC 7-19609-97367-6
Printed in China

Published by:

Wilderness Press
1200 5th Street
Berkeley, CA 94710
(800) 443-7227
www.wildernesspress.com

Grand Canyon Association
PO Box 399
Grand Canyon, AZ 86023-0399
(800) 858-2808
www.grandcanyon.org

Library of Congress Cataloging-in-Publication Data
    Miller, Steve, 1940-
    The grand : the Colorado River in the Grand Canyon, a photo journey /
by Steve Miller. p. cm. Includes index.
    ISBN 0-89997-367-1
    1. Grand Canyon (Ariz.)--Pictorial works. 2. Colorado River
(Colo.-Mexico)--Pictorial works. I. Title.

    F788.M55 2005
    917.91'32'00222--dc22
    2005047057

front cover and flap, left to right
Unkar Rapid at Mile 72.5; Point Hansbrough and President Harding Rapid at Mile 44; stream in Olo Canyon at Mile 145.5

ii
On the tongue of Hermit Rapid at Mile 95

iv–v
Sunset view to the east from camp at Mile 74

vi–vii
On the tongue of Lava Falls Rapid, right run, at Mile 179

ix
Downstream view at Mile 162

x
Basalt columns are side-lit by the setting sun at Mile 183.

back flap and cover, left to right
Desert marigold; upper falls of Thunder River; Deer Creek Gorge

Table of Contents

A Note from
the Grand
Canyon Association

Green glassy tongue
Sliding into chaos
Inevitability

These words met paper after I ran Crystal Rapid for the first time in the depths of the Grand Canyon. When you run whitewater, you must respect the river—both the power of the moving water and the amount of water running over myriad rocks. Hydrologists analyze the forces that are created by these conditions—predicting the way water should react—but the reality of the river-running experience is much more visceral. It is just you, the water, and the rocks—your fragile envelope of flesh and bones is by far the weakest of the trio.

There is tremendous power in moving water; even the most experienced Colorado River runners pull to the shore above major rapids to scout the water ahead. They know every run is different, that you can never take a run for granted. Water levels vary, and new rocks may have been pushed into the flow. As the raw power of the massive waves knots your stomach, you seek a mental path through the maelstrom. Do you enter river right or left? Where are the big holes? Which run gives you the best chance of coming through upright? Decisions are made, you tighten the straps on your life vest, and you move forward. The deafening roar of the surging water reminds you that this is some of the biggest whitewater in North America. You position your raft in the calm water above the rapid so it will enter the rapid at the exact starting point you have planned. You strengthen your grip on the oars as you slide down the tongue into the current, relinquishing yourself to the full control of the river.

As the executive director of the Grand Canyon Association, I have the opportunity to lead an organization that exists to help people learn and understand more about this magical place, which was carved by the Colorado River. The majority of the association's revenue comes from the sale of educational materials in our stores within Grand Canyon National Park. We use the proceeds from these sales to support education and science at the park. We operate a field institute, provide community lectures, publish and distribute free literature to park visitors, and work with people like author and photographer Steve Miller to bring you top-quality books like this one. In all of these endeavors, our goals are to illuminate and inspire you about the wonders of the canyon. We believe that if people perceive value in places like the Grand Canyon, they will protect and preserve such public lands for generations yet unborn.

This is a unique book; its pages will transport you through the inner canyon of the greatest natural wonder on Earth, and you will see things that are usually seen only by river runners. Through Steve Miller's images, you can share in this experience. And by making the decision to purchase this beautiful book, you can help support the very resources you are viewing: A portion of the proceeds from the sale of this book is returned to the Grand Canyon Association in support of the park.

So come to the inner canyon; see the delicate plants and animals that live in this harsh environment; let your view be framed by soaring walls of ancient rock thousands of feet high; see the reflection of glowing walls in glassy, calm waters; and feel the power of massive rapids. We invite you to join us where humans can visit, but nature still holds the high card. Enjoy!

—Brad L. Wallis, Executive Director, GCA

Grander than Grand

Any description or discussion of the Grand Canyon risks immediate verbal inflation, with adjectives piled on top of adjectives, superlatives on top of superlatives, and metaphors stretched so large they lose their hold on our imagination. The Grand Canyon is grander than our attempts to take it in.

The Grand Canyon isn't really an accurate name for this 6000-foot-deep, 277-mile-long canyon snaking across the high desert country of Arizona. It's an understatement. If we called it the Grandest Canyon, it would still be an understatement.

All we can do is stop talking about the Grand, and live it. Walk to the canyon's rim and look over the edge into a geological fantasy that drops and dives and twists and soars. Way down there is a muddy brushstroke of a river, so small, so far away, that the first Spanish conquistadors to glimpse it from the rim guessed that it was only a few feet across. They were wrong, of course. But scale in this canyon is not a given.

Understanding in this canyon is not a given, either. The Grand Canyon is a mysterious, unchanging, ever-changing place. Today we have just as hard a time wrapping our minds around this exquisite eroded painted gash in the planet's skin as those early Spanish explorers. We have read all the geology guidebooks, and we still can't quite believe what we are seeing. And seeing is only the beginning—but what a beginning!—because the Grand demands more. We have to hike it, to drop down those snaking trails, twisting through polychrome rock and dust, to follow those dotted lines, down, down, down, thousands of feet down, to the river, to that other world. We are foreigners on leave from everyday reality.

Ultimately there's no choice but to extend that leave. The only way to truly gain perspective in this vast canyon is to boat down the Grand. My friend, Herb Lewis, a dynamic octogenarian and landscape photographer currently preparing for his fourth river trip down the Grand with his great-grandson, put it perfectly when he told me: "Rafting down the Grand is a once-in-a-lifetime experience that one should do as often as possible." Herb is right. Each one of us has a boat trip down the Grand Canyon waiting just around the bend.

I've rafted the Grand twice—more times on the river than I deserve. And yet it's never enough. I'll never forget Steve Miller's voice on the phone, asking if I could get away for a private 18-day trip down the Grand. How long did it take me to say yes? A nanosecond? I can't remember, but it wasn't long.

I can remember every rapid, every evening, every campsite and beach, and every hike. I remember Steve pointing out the trickiest wave in a tricky rapid, Steve disappearing overhead up a ragged rope into the mouth of Olo Canyon, Steve giving geology lessons disguised as casual banter. I also remember the gaudy sunsets and the saturated pink predawn skies we later learned were due to the explosion of Mt. Pinatubo in the Phillipines, a half a world and a hundred worlds away. And I clearly remember the takeout, 18 days later, deflating the rafts and packing up the gear with one thought foremost in my mind: Why can't we go back up to Lees Ferry and start again?

I was lucky to experience the Grand with Steve Miller. Years ago, Steve, a mountain-climbing companion, joined me in my wonderfully misspent youth on the crags of Yosemite and Chamonix. Years later, he became my guide-initiator to the timeless adventure of the Grand. Everyone knows something about the Grand Canyon, but very few actually know the Grand, and fewer still know it well. Steve Miller is one of those happy few. Now Steve will be your guide, as he was mine. He understands that the Grand—the full experience—can't be condensed into a few words, or even a multitude of words. Short of pushing off into the cold canyon current on a warm Arizona morning below Glen Canyon Dam, photos convey the feel and flow and pulse of this grand river better than anything else.

A great guide makes the journey come alive and gives you everything you need to make it your own. If you are lucky enough to share a raft with him, Steve Miller does just that—bringing to life an explosive stretch of western whitewater or showing you the serenity of the still water in some cliff-shaded horseshoe meander. As a fine photographer and consummate river insider, he also does that in the pages of this visual guide to the Grand. It's a Grand trip, a Grand gift—enjoy it and savor it. Thanks to this book, we will all be able to repeat this once-in-a-lifetime experience a few extra times.

—Lito Tejada-Flores was born at 13,000 feet in the Bolivian Andes and has spent much of his life in high places. He has shared his passion for mountain adventure in documentary films as well as a variety of books, on wilderness skiing, kayaking, and, most recently, in *Breakthrough on the New Skis*, on downhill skiing.

Preface

We met at a dance, at the hotel on the North Rim of the Grand Canyon. Dorothy was 15—just like me. The moon was full. We left the dance and wandered out on a trail that led toward an overlook. The trail followed the narrow crest of a promontory, leading us into the moonlit immensity of the Canyon. A curved railing brought us to a stop, and we turned to each other and kissed.

My family and I left early the next morning. Big mule deer stood belly-deep in mist. Close by, a flock of wild turkeys could barely be seen. It was 1955—my family's first and only trip "Out West." On that same trip, we caught cutthroat trout in Yellowstone, rainbow trout in Glacier National Park, and gazed at the gleaming walls of Yosemite. What a smorgasbord for a city kid! My mother says that they lost me to the West on that trip.

Did I ever see Dorothy again? Of course not. But would I return to the Grand Canyon? You bet!

Since that turning point, my active life has centered on outdoor pursuits, with adventure and nature photography a constant element. It started with rock climbing, mountaineering, kayaking, rafting, fly-fishing, and skiing, and it continues much the same.

In 1971, I was teaching skiing at Aspen Highlands in Colorado. My ski school supervisor, Dave Farny, ran a summer adventure camp outside of Aspen, and he told me that some of his counselors were going to do a Grand trip in June. "Doing the Grand" is shorthand for running the Colorado River in the Grand Canyon. My girlfriend, Marguerite, and I talked ourselves onto the trip.

It was my first river trip of any sort. It was also the occasion of my first flip, which is a mishap similar to driving a car into a ditch. It happened in Crystal Rapid, one of the two hardest rapids on the river. Marguerite and I were seated in the back of the largest raft. The boat hit a huge wave head-on. As I saw the bow climbing for the sky, I took one last photo with my underwater camera and then leaped off backward. After freeing herself from a rope entanglement, Marguerite surfaced, and we made it to shore in one piece. About an hour later, the raft was restored to right-side up, and we continued.

Very soon after returning from the Grand, I took up kayaking, and that eventually led back to rafting. Around this time, I was freelancing for Outward Bound-type programs for criminal offenders, known generically as "hoods in the woods." For three years in the early '70s, I taught anthropology and chaired the Department of Physical Recreation at New Mexico Tech, in Socorro, where I created and directed a curriculum of outdoor adventure activities. For this and other programs, I designed long hikes in the Grand Canyon. By the end of the '70s, my wife, Kathy, and I were working for the Southwest Outward Bound School,

in Santa Fe, New Mexico. The course content included rafting on local white-water sections of the Rio Grande.

My next opportunity to get on the Grand—and Kathy's first—came in 1979, in the form of an Outward Bound training trip operated by Arizona Raft Adventures. It was in March, and it was cold. (Those were the days of sneakers and wool socks.) But we met some fine boatmen and -women, and Kathy fell head over heels for the Grand.

In 1980, Kathy and I founded New Wave Rafting Company in Santa Fe, and we returned to the Grand in 1980, 1981, and 1983. The '83 trip was the same year that Lake Powell came very close to overtopping Glen Canyon Dam. Unanticipated spring snowstorms had overfilled the lake in June, and the dam operators were forced to make emergency releases that approached 100,000 cubic feet per second (cfs). These huge releases caused havoc on the river and damaged the dam. In September, the river was running 40,000 cfs and provided more than enough excitement.

On that same trip, we ran into a film crew that was re-creating Major John Wesley Powell's trips of exploration. They had built wooden replicas of Powell's boats, and they had hired the best guides on the river to row them. Nevertheless, the boats were extremely tippy. We first watched them run North Canyon Rapid, an easy one, losing only one boatman overboard. Later, their filming held us up at other locations, but they paid us off in pastrami—better than money in the Grand Canyon. Our final encounter with the crew was at Crystal Rapid. The guides had refused to take the Powell boats through Crystal, which is not only one of the

two most difficult rapids in the Grand Canyon but also the single most feared rapid. A "swim" in Crystal can subject you to a bruising (or worse) encounter with the Island, a midstream collection of semisubmerged boulders. Instead, they loaded the Powell boats onto the large motorized rafts that were supporting the filming effort.

In September of 1987 and 1988, after our rafting season had ended in New Mexico, Kathy and I worked for Arizona Raft Adventures as baggage boatmen. Baggage boatmen are supposed to carry only baggage, as one would imagine, but it didn't always work out that way, especially when we were mopping up after a flip.

In 1989, we did an Arizona Raft Adventures "fam" trip—a discounted familiarization trip for travel agents. We were to do the first half only, but partway down we ran into another Arizona Raft Adventures trip. This one was a women's trip staffed by friends of ours. Kathy, naturally, got an invite to continue with them. I hiked out. Private trips followed in 1991, 1995, 1999, and 2003.

I was 31 when I first ran the Grand, and I was 63 on my most recent trip in 2003. What is it that keeps bringing me back? I hope the photos in this book will provide a more compelling answer to this question than my words can. But let me try anyway.

First and foremost, there is no landscape more stunning or more extraordinary. Add to that the raw excitement of running the awesome rapids of the Colorado. Then consider what it is like to be outdoors for weeks at a time—neither able to escape from bad weather within the walls of a house, nor able to escape to television, movies, or other distractions. From one day to the next, you are likely to be too hot, too cold, too damp, too dry; chilled, sunburned, or blistered; suffering from bruises, stubbed toes, cracked fingertips, or a sore back—but still glorying in the place, the experience, the Canyon.

Every day you're on hand for sunrise and sunset, and every night you're there for the changes in the moon. Except when the clouds rush in to blot them out, the stars are as brilliant as you've ever seen. And the storms always come, but then go, leaving rainbows in their wakes. Much of the magic comes from your literal immersion into the river and Canyon. You are in it, enclosed by it—there is nowhere else. You have left civilization behind, as though it were a dream.

Day by day, the realities of living in the wild bring home the reality of being in the Canyon—this stupendous, outrageous, all-encompassing place. As it sinks in, as you adapt, your initially hurried pace slackens. You're in the Canyon, all 200-plus miles of it. What's the hurry?

As to those persons you have chosen to accompany, or who accompany you— well…you are, really *are,* with them. There is no getting away. And if someone proves bothersome, you will want to wring his or her neck by the end of the trip. But if you're all compatible, the trip becomes a nonstop party. You become, then, a band of nomads, living, sharing, and endeavoring together in the wilderness. You can hardly find that anywhere else.

By the end of the trip, you are so accustomed to this way of life that

you are ready to go right back to Lees Ferry and start down the Colorado again—anything but having to go home. And arrival back home produces predictable culture shock, which can last for a week or more.

These are some of the things that don't show in photos. What the photos do show is this place that is like no other, and that keeps bringing me back.

I have, at the time of this writing, an upcoming "shoulder-season" launch for early March. I took this less-than-desirable date for fear that I might otherwise not be able to get back on the Grand. (In recent years, private permits have

been hard to obtain.) Of course, there is always the chance that the unexpected phone call will come. A friend will announce that his or her number has come up for next year, and would we like to go? Or, you, the reader, might call, telling me that a group of photographers is booking a Grand trip and would like to pay my way, in exchange for photo instruction. I'm sitting by the phone.

above:

Seated behind two oarsmen, I snapped this picture as the raft lifted up, on its way to flipping end-over-end. Crystal Rapid, June 1971

This funnel is found at riverside downstream of Glen Canyon Dam and is representative of what was lost in Glen Canyon.

Introduction

At 277 miles long, 6000 feet deep, and 10 miles wide, the Grand Canyon of Arizona is one of the seven natural wonders of the world. Beginning at Lees Ferry (Mile 0), it cuts through a vast uplifted area called the Colorado Plateau before it ends at the Grand Wash Cliffs (Mile 277). Today, practically the entire canyon is administered by the National Park Service, with the main portion designated as Grand Canyon National Park. Three Indian reservations—the Navajo, Hualapai, and Havasupai—are found within, or along the rim of, the geologic Grand Canyon and abut Grand Canyon National Park.

The overwhelming majority of visitors to the park arrive at one or the other rim, most often the South Rim. But from either rim, the remarkable views into the Canyon are what have put the Grand Canyon on the map.

I have spent many hours on the rims, especially at sunrise and sunset, when the low sun reddens the already warm and rich colors of the rock strata, and long shadows bring out the symmetry of the Canyon formations. Invariably, whenever I gaze into the Canyon from the rim, my wish is to go down there. So, for me, the rims have usually represented starting and finishing points of hikes, all of which have taken me to the Colorado River, far below.

From the rim, one can barely make out the Colorado River. Literally miles away, the river appears to be little more than a creek. And though this is certainly not the case, the Colorado is not, in fact, a large-volume river like the Hudson or the Columbia. But it is a long river. Not only is it the architect of the Grand Canyon, it is also the major river system of the central and southern Rocky Mountains and of the desert Southwest. The Colorado and its major tributary, the Green, originate in the high mountains of Colorado and Wyoming. Both above and below their confluence in Utah, these rivers have cut additional canyon systems that, all told, extend for hundreds of miles upstream of the Grand Canyon.

The two rivers meet in Utah's Canyonlands National Park. Downstream of this point, the Colorado has carved the imposing Cataract Canyon, with rapids equal to those of the Grand Canyon. Below Cataract Canyon is (or was) the incomparable Glen Canyon—called "the place no one knew" by the photographer Eliot Porter, in a Sierra Club book of the same name. The book was published in 1963, the same year that all but 15 miles of the 170-mile-long Glen Canyon began to disappear under the still waters of Lake Powell, the reservoir backed up by Glen Canyon Dam. The reservoir is named for Major John Wesley Powell, the explorer of the Green and Colorado rivers. The remaining 15 miles of Glen Canyon are found downstream of the dam, ending at Lees Ferry and the start of the Grand Canyon.

In its entire course through the Grand Canyon, the Colorado is bridged at rim level only once, by Navajo Bridge at Mile 4. Only one road reaches the river in the Grand Canyon. This dirt road, on the Hualapai Indian Reservation, meets the river at Diamond Creek at Mile 226. It floods often and requires constant maintenance. It is sometimes closed for days at a time.

Below Diamond Creek, the last 40 miles of the Colorado River in the Grand Canyon is subject to inundation by Lake Mead, the reservoir backed up by Hoover Dam. At full pool, the lake reaches to approximately Mile 236, drowning several of the Colorado River's largest rapids. When drought causes the lake's surface elevation to drop, a wasteland of sand and mud is left behind. Lovers of the Grand Canyon very much regret this loss.

Despite the indignities that these two dams have imposed on the Colorado River, it *is* the architect of the Grand Canyon and will continue in that role long after the dams wear to rubble. There is no better way, therefore, to experience and appreciate the Grand Canyon than to spend some time on, or at least along, the river. There are three ways to do this: by hiking or riding a mule into the Canyon, or via the Colorado River.

Hiking will always remain an attractive and rewarding endeavor, with unlimited destinations available, while riding a mule into the canyon is limited to just three trails. The Colorado River, on the other hand, provides access to the entirety of the inner canyon, and that portion of the inner canyon that lies adjacent to the river—the river corridor—holds the greatest abundance of the Canyon's treasures.

First among those treasures is the Inner Gorge, which is present for a significant percentage of the Canyon's length. The Inner Gorge is composed of ancient and durable metamorphic rocks that vary considerably in appearance from the stratified sedimentary rocks above. At river level, these metamorphic rocks have been sculpted and polished in a fashion seen in few other places.

There is no end to the surprises that await the first-time river traveler in the Grand Canyon. The Canyon is incised by many side canyons, some of which support perennial streams. Many of the side canyons have sections that have been eroded into exotically narrow and convoluted slot canyons. Those with perennial streams are characterized by smoothly polished rock, waterfalls, pools, and hanging gardens of flowers and ferns—made all the more fantastic because of the desert surroundings. Elsewhere, larger streams have carved gorges and more open lush valleys along their courses. Some streams issue from caves, often as waterfalls, creating vertical oases. Springs are found in side canyons and along shorelines, in a variety of forms. Caves, Indian ruins, rock art, fossils, and other unique features are also found along the river. It would take literally years of hiking to get to all of the extraordinary places that a river trip makes available in a matter of days or weeks.

And then, of course, there is the experience of the river itself. If the river just flowed placidly through the Grand Canyon (as was the case in Glen Canyon), it would suffice to enchant, as only moving water can do. And, in fact, it flows placidly for most of its trip through the Grand Canyon. Every so often, however, the river approaches the mouth of a tributary canyon—a side canyon.

Found at the mouth of practically every side canyon is a delta, a protruding assemblage of mud, silt, sand, rocks, and boulders that constricts the river channel. Like water spurting from the nozzle on a hose, the river speeds up as it flows through the constricted channel. Boulders that extend into the narrowed river channel complete the picture. When exposed, these boulders constitute obstacles to navigation. Rafts can get pinned and then swamped against the upstream sides of boulders, which is called a "wrap." When submerged under a few feet of water, boulders create pour-overs, which are, in fact, waterfalls off the downstream side of the boulder that can flip a raft. When more completely submerged, boulders create holes (troughs) and large waves that can also flip rafts. You have, in short, a rapid. Most, but not all, rapids in the Grand Canyon are thus found at the mouths of side canyons. Other rapids, but not many, are created by bedrock obstructions.

The deltas that form the rapids owe their existence to the rampaging flash floods and occasional debris flows that regularly occur in the southwestern canyon country. Summer monsoon rains and winter El Niño deluges run off large expanses of slickrock and quickly collect in arroyos that feed into canyon systems. Mud, silt, sand, and rocks are swept along by the advancing waters. Heavy rains that soak steep and unstable hillsides cause massive slope failures. These huge slumps of saturated soil, rocks, and boulders become debris flows that are as much solid as liquid, moving downstream like a slurry of concrete. Flash floods and debris flows further erode the courses of the canyons. Then

they are finally violently ejected into the Colorado River. When the storms subside, the work of these floods can be seen. At any time, a massive flood or debris flow can turn a small delta into a large one, and a small rapid into a newly menacing monster that becomes the talk of the rafting season.

Ninety-five of the rapids in the Colorado River are named, and each is rated on a 1-to-10 scale. Were this river found elsewhere, the quality of the whitewater experience alone would put it in the top ranks of North American rivers. It's very much worth doing, irrespective of its location in the recesses of the Grand Canyon. But it *is* in the heart and *is* the heart of the Grand Canyon.

River running in the Grand Canyon began in earnest after World War II, when military surplus rubber rafts of different designs became readily available. Smaller rafts were rowed, while the larger rafts, or pontoons, were equipped with outboard motors. These served the dual purpose of carrying more passengers and allowing for faster trips through the Canyon. Today, river runners use motorized rafts, oar- or paddle-powered rafts, dories, kayaks, and even riverboards (about the size of a surfboard!). Most outfitted trips take place in the warmer months, but private (self-guided) boaters go at all times of the year. Half trips are made possible by entering or exiting the Canyon via the Bright Angel Trail between Phantom Ranch and the South Rim.

Since 1964, when Glen Canyon Dam began operations and the Wilderness Act was passed, two environmental issues have come to the fore.

First, the very presence and continuing operation of Glen Canyon Dam alters the river ecosystem. The lake traps sediment, which leads to the loss of beaches and backwater habitat. Fluctuating releases intended to optimize electrical power supply create artificial tides that further erode beaches and are a constant source of irritation to river runners. The cold water that is released into the river from deep within Lake Powell has led to the decline of native fishes. And the absence of natural flooding promotes the growth of undesirable nonnative vegetation. As a result, the Colorado River has largely been stripped of its natural character and there are now increasing calls for decommissioning the dam.

The second issue concerns the presence of motorized travel along the river corridor, in the form of outboard-powered rafts and, at one locale, helicopter transport of rafting guests. Motorized travel has so far held up wilderness designation for the entire inner canyon of the Grand Canyon, in so far as wilderness, by definition, is a landscape free of motors.

Wilderness designation would provide the highest level of legislative protection to the Grand Canyon, and wilderness advocates feel it is imperative that the inner canyon of the Grand Canyon be so protected—and for good reason. In the mid-'60s, only very strenuous efforts on the part of the Sierra Club and its allies saved the Grand Canyon itself from being dammed. Tunneling at one of the two proposed dam sites, at Mile 39, is still evident and serves as a reminder to Grand Canyon river runners that, without full wilderness protection, the Canyon is not yet secure from the threat of dams and other

mechanized intrusions. Advocates for wilderness protection of the inner canyon of the Grand Canyon note that running the Grand is the greatest remaining wilderness adventure in the lower 48 states and should be accorded the protection it deserves.

In defense of motorized rafting, outfitters contend that much of the public demands the level of safety, speed, convenience, and comfort that the larger, motorized boats provide. It is also the case that motorized boating has a history of more than 50 years on the river.

These and related issues have now been debated for decades. Thousands of people have attended public meetings and many more have written letters. There is probably no other natural place in this country that has generated more advocacy and argument. And no wonder. We are talking about running the Colorado River in the Grand Canyon—the most sought-after wilderness river trip in the United States, if not the world.

My wife, Kathy, and I are looking forward to our next scheduled launch, still some years in the future. We hope to have three generations of family on this trip. Could there be a more desirable destination for such a communal adventure than running the Grand—to be able to spend weeks together, sharing the unrivaled majesty of the Grand Canyon and the excitement of the Colorado River's rapids? I doubt it.

Let this book, this photo journey down the Colorado in the Grand Canyon, fire your imagination, until such time as you, too, make it your own. I hope to see you there.

High and Dry at Soap Creek
Mile 11.2.

above:

These river runners, at their first camp in the Canyon, are learning the hard way about the Colorado River's "tides."

right:

Fly-fishing for rainbow trout below Glen Canyon Dam

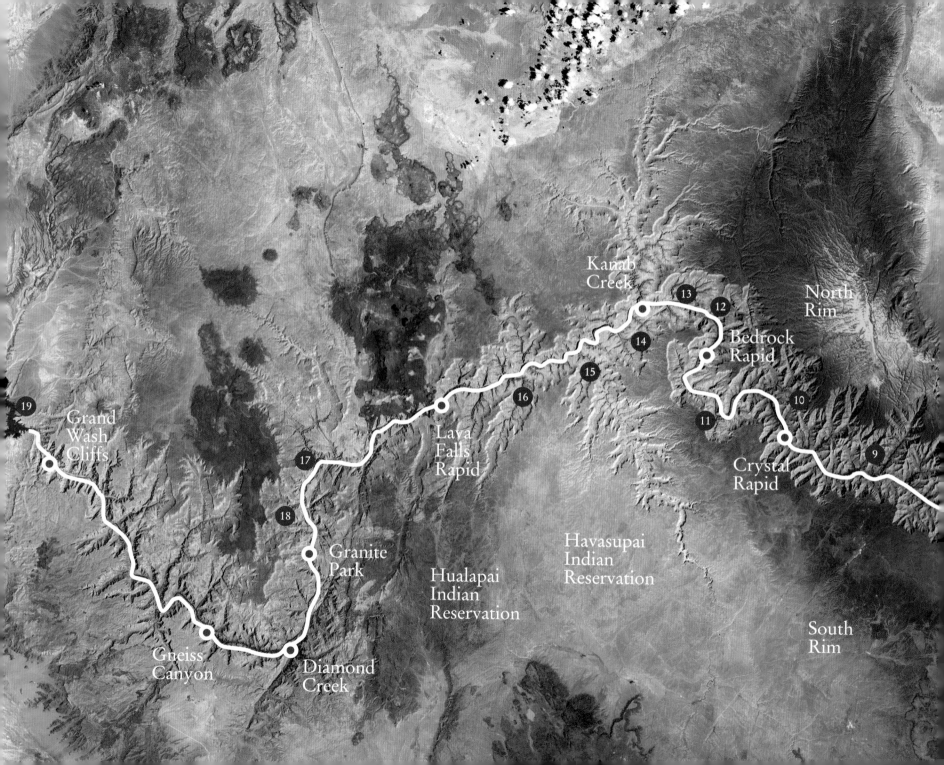

Kanab
Creek

North
Rim

13

12

Bedrock
Rapid

14

15

10

16

11

9

Crystal
Rapid

Lava
Falls
Rapid

17

Havasupai
Indian
Reservation

Grand
Wash
Cliffs

19

18

Granite
Park

Hualapai
Indian
Reservation

South
Rim

Gneiss
Canyon

Diamond
Creek

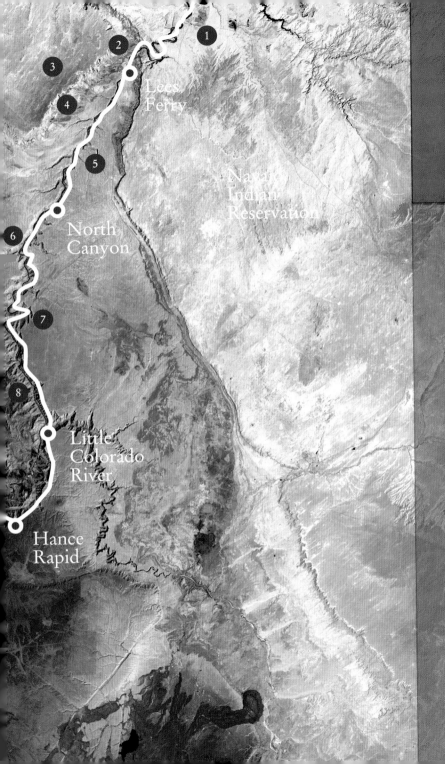

Lees
Ferry

Navajo
Indian
Reservation

North
Canyon

Little
Colorado
River

Hance
Rapid

The Grand Canyon
of the Colorado River

1. Glen Canyon Dam

2. Paria River

3. Paria Plateau

4. Vermilion Cliffs

5. House Rock Rapid

6. South Canyon

7. Point Hansbrough

8. Nankoweap Creek

9. Bright Angel Creek

10. Shinumo Creek

11. Elves Chasm

12. Tapeats Creek

13. Deer Creek

14. Olo Canyon

15. Havasu Canyon

16. National Canyon

17. Parashant Wash

18. 205 Mile Rapid

19. Lake Mead

Marble Canyon

Miles 0-27

The first 61 miles of the Grand Canyon, from Lees Ferry to the confluence with the Little Colorado River, is known as Marble Canyon. Marble Canyon can be considered to have two sections—the first, miles 0 through 27, contains some vigorous rapids, and the second, miles 28 through 61, has some of the best scenery in the Grand Canyon.

As river travelers penetrate the ever-deepening canyon, they become acquainted with the layers of rock that form the upper-most cliffs and slopes of the Grand Canyon. Each layer appears first at river level and then ascends slowly overhead. The rock layers in this first part of Marble Canyon are, from top to bottom: the Kaibab Formation (a.k.a. the Kaibab Limestone), the Toroweap Formation (varied sedimentary rocks), the Coconino Sandstone, the Hermit Formation (a.k.a. the Hermit Shale), the Supai Group (sandstone and other sedimentary rocks), and the Redwall Limestone.

In this section, river runners encounter the first of the Colorado's many rapids–some mild, some moderate, and some quite challenging, but all on a scale that impresses.

North Canyon, at Mile 20.5, is the first of many extraordinary side canyons that together constitute one of the greatest treasures of the river corridor. The stretch of rapids known as the Roaring Twenties, beginning with North Canyon Rapid at Mile 20.5, leads into the gorge of the Redwall Limestone, for which Marble Canyon is named.

This section of Marble Canyon ends at Mile 27, with its fluted limestone.

opposite page:
Early morning mist on the Colorado River at Lees Ferry, Mile 0

Sunrise on the Vermilion Cliffs at Lees Ferry

Lees Ferry
Mile 0

At Lees Ferry, the put-in for the Grand, Arizona Raft Adventures guests receive a safety talk before embarking. Motorized (larger) and oar- or paddle-powered (smaller) rafts are lined up to receive participants. At the far end of the beach, a private (noncommercial) party prepares to launch. In this downstream view, the Vermilion Cliffs are seen on photo right, forming the western horizon.

The Launch Ramp at Lees Ferry
Miles 0 to 1.75

The launch ramp for trips both up and down the Colorado River is named for John D. Lee, who established a ferry at this locale sometime after his arrival in 1871. The Lees Ferry launch ramp is the departure point for trips downriver through the Grand Canyon, and upriver into the remaining 15 miles of Glen Canyon.

The site of the ferry crossing was dictated by the lay of the land. The geologic transition from one canyon to another provided an opening to the river that allowed wagons, and now cars, an easy approach from the west.

The scenery at Lees Ferry is outstanding. The southern flank of the massive Glen Canyon sandstone formation forms a colorful sloping cliff to the north. Directly to the west is the extensive canyon system of the Paria River. Bordering the Paria River Canyon on the south is the Paria Plateau, which breaks off as the imposing Vermilion Cliffs, a feature that forms the western skyline for many miles. Across the river to the east and south are the jagged Echo Peaks and the monolithic Echo Cliffs, on the Navajo Reservation.

Lees Ferry, also known as "the Ferry" to river guides, is a magical place. If its splendor is overlooked by anxious river runners,

it's because it is still civilization, compared to the long-awaited wilderness glories of the Grand, just downstream.

The anticipation and excitement of arriving at and readying for the launch at the Ferry cannot be overstated. Whether commercial guest, commercial guide, or private river runner, large amounts of time, and/or energy, and/or money have been invested to get to the banks of the Colorado. This is not just your ordinary vacation, after all. This is the Grand, unequivocally the greatest river trip in the world.

As can be seen in the photo, the Colorado runs crystal clear at Lees Ferry. The often

muddy Paria River, however, enters just downstream of the launch ramp. If muddy, it immediately dirties the Colorado. If not, a flooding tributary farther downstream may do so. When there are no storms in the area, the Colorado may run clear all the way to Lake Mead. The Colorado runs clear because of the presence of Glen Canyon Dam, located 15 miles upstream of Lees Ferry. The sediment load of the Colorado River settles out in the upper end of Lake Powell, the name given by the Bureau of Reclamation to the impounded waters held back by the dam. The lake water is gin-clear when released back into the channel of the Colorado River below the dam.

The Launch Ramp
at Lees Ferry (cont.)
Miles 0 to 1.75

right:

Up early to start rigging the boats at Lees Ferry launch ramp. No, not all that gear is going into only three boats. Another six boats remain to be inflated. (Photo by Peter Donahue)

below left:

Just around the first corner, at Mile 1.75, is a good place for lunch. The low cliff pictured at this site is the Kaibab, the rim-rock of the Grand Canyon. This layer and those beneath rise gradually to the south, eventually climbing from an elevation of 3000 feet at Lees Ferry to 8000 feet at the North Rim. The Canyon, therefore, deepens more as a result of this upward ascent of the layered sequence of rocks, and less as a result of the riverbed dropping. In effect, the Colorado River has cut the Grand Canyon through a huge dome of rock.

3 Mile Wash
below right:

Blooming prickly pear cactus and Mormon tea at the mouth of 3 Mile Wash

Navajo Bridge
Mile 4.5

below left:

Close under Navajo Bridge, the sheer rock wall seen behind the boat consists of the Toroweap Formation above, and the Coconino Sandstone below. The Coconino is seen here as angled layers. These angled layers were originally deposited on the steep faces of advancing sand dunes, which later hardened into sandstone. As can be seen in this photo, the upper surface of the Coconino was eroded flat prior to the subsequent marine deposition of sediments that hardened into the buff-colored Toroweap Formation. This contact is called an unconformity because the period of time during which the partial erosion of the Coconino took place is now missing from the geologic record. There is, in other words, a time gap at this contact.

above right:

California condors were released into the Vermilion Cliffs area in 1996 and frequent this uppermost stretch of the canyon.

below right:

This downstream view of the newer Navajo Bridge looks south onto the Navajo Reservation. The Echo Cliffs are on the eastern skyline.

Badger Creek Rapid
Mile 7.8

opposite page:

Badger Creek Rapid is the first large rapid in the Grand, and it is scouted from river left, which means to the left when looking downstream. (Likewise, river right is to the right as you're looking in the direction the river is flowing.) Large boulders are seen to the right of the raft in this low-water run. These boulders have been deposited into the river by debris flows originating in Badger Creek.

Badger Creek Rapid has an overall vertical drop of 15 feet and is rated 5-8 on a scale of 1 to 10. This range of ratings recognizes that the nature of the difficulties associated with this (and other) rapids depends on the water level. Nowadays, the magnitude of flows in the Colorado River below Glen Canyon Dam is completely a function of releases of lake water from the dam.

Typically, releases are greater during the day and lesser at night, to adjust to varying electrical power demands. Releases also vary by season and by idiosyncratic factors, such as

efforts to rebuild beaches and impede the breeding of trout, which are thought to be associated with the decline of native fish. So, while flows varied only by season (and the occasional short-lived flash flood) in pre-dam days, now they vary from hour to hour and day to day. Under normal operations, releases can vary by as much as 200 percent within a 24-hour period.

In this photo, the raft enters the rapid on the tongue, seen here as an unobstructed V-shaped pathway of smooth water. Ahead and to the right of the raft, on the right margin of the tongue, is a nasty hole created by a large subsurface rock. A hole this large can flip a boat of the size pictured. In the lower left-hand corner of the photo, to the left of the tongue, is a light gray rock that is just barely visible above the surface. A rafter who runs over such a sharp limestone rock risks ripping the floor of the boat.

Some hazards, such as the hole on the right, can easily be spotted on the approach to a rapid. Others are less obvious, such as the rock on the left. Discretion, therefore, dictates that, as a rule, one enters a rapid on the tongue. And discretion further dictates that a rafting party pull over to inspect a rapid

from the shore if no straightforward route can be seen on the approach. While Badger does have a tongue that can be spotted from upstream, the rapid is, nevertheless, big and intimidating. Those unfamiliar with the river will usually pull over on the left and climb a slope to get a complete view of the rapid.

Ten Mile Rock

Ten Mile Rock is a fallen slab standing on edge. To the right in this photo is a cliff of the three uppermost layers that appear throughout the Grand Canyon. From top to bottom, they are: the Kaibab Limestone, the Toroweap Formation, and the Coconino Sandstone. These are underlain by a slope of the soft Hermit Formation.

At 10 miles in, the Canyon is already approximately 500 feet deep, and deepening at a rate of 50 feet per mile. But the riverbed is only dropping at an average of less than 10 feet per mile, which means that the rock strata are inclining upward at the rate of about 40 feet per mile.

Here, the river has cut a channel into the upwardly ascending layers of a massive dome of rock. Ten Mile Rock is at the lower margin of that dome. The big question, of course, is how does a river cut into a dome? The probable answer is that when the river first established its channel, the topography of the region was then vastly different from the topography today. It is currently thought that the river cut a channel into a flat-lying deposit that, at the time, sat above the dome. Having cut through this deposit, the river continued to cut downward into the dome. Eventually, the original overlying deposit eroded away, leaving the river channel entrenched in the dome.

This is but one hypothesis for the cutting of the canyon. Additional study will certainly lead to a better understanding of this geologic puzzle.

Soap Creek Rapid
Mile 11.2

above:

Soap Creek Rapid is formed by the delta at the mouth of Soap Creek, on river right. The boulders that extend from the main body of the delta into the river obstruct navigation, both as exposed rocks or sub-surface rocks that create breaking waves and holes. Waves are also caused by the discharge of energy as the fast-moving water rebounds off the bottom and off the slower-moving water in the pool below the rapid. Soap Creek Rapid has a drop of 16 feet and is rated 5-7. A cliff of the reddish Hermit Formation is seen on river left, in the background.

below right:

On the tongue of Soap Creek Rapid

Mile 12.3 Camp

opposite page:

At Mile 12.3 camp, the rafts are pulled up to a shelving beach that is insurance against stranding by low water, which will occur at night and persist until the morning release of water reaches this point, 27 miles below the dam.

A guide sleeping in the blue-and-white tent seen here erected aboard one of the rafts will stay alert through the night. When the raft tilts, that will indicate to the guide that the water has dropped and left the raft inclined on the sand. At that point, the guide will shove all the rafts back into the river.

Guides learn by experience which beaches allow for this option.

In the background, a storm has created a rainbow, and the cloud-filtered light gilds the cliff of Kaibab, Toroweap, and Coconino.

The Gorge of the Supai

Mile 13

above left:

At Mile 13, the river enters a gorge formed by the first member of the Supai Group of sandstones and limestones, the cliff-forming Esplanade Sandstone. Harder rocks are cliff-forming; softer rocks such as the overlying Hermit Formation are slope-forming.

Sheer Wall Rapid

Miles 14 to 16

above right:

Sheer Wall Rapid, at Mile 14.3, is found at the mouth of Tanner Wash. In the Grand Canyon region, a wash is a watercourse created by intermittent flows, usually the result of thunderstorms. A drainage called a creek may also enjoy only intermittent flows or flow perennially in only a few places. Therefore, not every creek actually flows into the Colorado. Sheer Wall Rapid has a drop of 9 feet and is rated 2-3.

below right:

Great blue herons are often seen along the river corridor.

House Rock Rapid
Mile 16.9

"Pull like mad!" In this photo, our friend Lito Tejada-Flores is urging my wife, Kathy, to get to the right of a very large, breaking wave, which she succeeded in doing. House Rock Rapid is the first difficult rapid encountered so far, with a drop of 10 feet and a solid rating of 7-9.

As the river bends left around the delta at the mouth of Rider Canyon, the current is directed hard up against a ledgy cliff of the Supai on river left. As a river channel bends, the water in the river runs straight until it deflects off the outside bank of the bend, which means that a raft would likely strike that outside bank in the absence of efforts to move the raft otherwise. This leftward push of the current aims your raft directly at, first, a large breaking wave capable of flipping a boat and, second, a very deep and scary hole.

The rapid can be scouted to the very bottom by scrambling (carefully) on ledges on river left. Unless you do so, you cannot appreciate the size of the wave and hole that await a mistake on the part of whoever is at the oars.

18 Mile Wash and Boulder Narrows

left:

Between October 1 and April 30, boaters can gather wood and enjoy campfires. Here, on a cold morning, our campfire heats both us and our dishwater (and helps us save on bottled gas). In order to keep the beach clean, the fire is contained in a fire pan. The ashes will be deposited into the garbage, all of which will be removed from the Canyon. Some of the rafts are stranded on the beach, but these will be easily returned to the water, because the beach is steep and not too rocky. The water is clear, making for good trout fishing. When the water is muddy, it seems that the trout just stop feeding.

right:

Boulder Narrows, at Mile 18.5, consists of one huge boulder that divides the river. Atop this rock is driftwood from a massive flood that occurred in 1957, prior to the construction of Glen Canyon Dam. North Canyon is coming up!

North Canyon
Mile 20.5

opposite page:
This somewhat abstract photo shows shaded pools in the bedrock of North Canyon reflecting brilliantly sunlit canyon walls. The difference in texture between the two surfaces can throw the eye off.

above:
As you enter the slot canyon portion of North Canyon, you must wade this pool to continue farther. The saturated color of the Supai walls is due to the light reflected from the walls above. This strong but indirect light intensifies color.

opposite page left:
Looking down the slot toward the main pool

opposite page right:
Pools reflect the sunlit walls

above left:
Canyon tree frogs mimic the color of the rock they cling to and depend on this camouflage to avoid detection.

above right:
Chuckwalla on a shoulder

below right:
The desert bighorn sheep that graze at riverside are easily approached by quietly drifting boats.

MILES 0-27

Mile 21

left:

An overhang in the Supai at Mile 21 shades these two boats that missed the eddy at North Canyon. In an eddy, which forms behind anything that obstructs a flow (whether liquid or gas), the current reverses and flows back toward the obstruction. Eddies are found below shoreline protrusions or boulders or behind midstream boulders.

Almost invariably, a large eddy occurs below a rapid on the delta side of the river. The upstream flow in the eddy can be in strong contrast to the downstream flow of the main current, creating a shear zone, which may display powerful whirlpools. The whirlpools can grab and spin boats and submerge kayaks. The shear zone, or eddyline, can be difficult to penetrate and is often the reason why boats that intend to come to shore miss eddies and must continue downstream. This is particularly unfortunate if the eddy missed was at the intended campsite, as was the case here.

The Roaring Twenties
Miles 20.5 to 25.3

right:

The Roaring Twenties begin with North Canyon Rapid, at Mile 20.5, followed by 21 Mile Rapid and 23 Mile Rapid (a.k.a. Indian Dick Rapid). Here, at Indian Dick Rapid, the low gray cliff directly ahead and downstream of the boat is the first appearance of the Redwall Limestone, destined to become the single most prominent cliff in the Grand Canyon.

But why is it called the Redwall if it's gray? With the exception of places where the Redwall Limestone is scoured by waterborne abrasives, either at riverside or where storm runoff pours off cliffs, the Redwall has been stained by seepage from the very red Hermit Formation that overlies it. The Hermit also stains the intervening Supai, but, unlike the Redwall, the Supai was red to begin with. Indian Dick Rapid drops 5 feet and is rated 2-5.

The Roaring Twenties (cont.)
Miles 20.5 to 25.3

left:

24.5 Mile Rapid is the first difficult rapid of the series. It drops 9 feet and is rated 5-7. The raft is seen passing to the right of a large hole.

opposite page left:

Evening light at Mile 23.5 camp

Entering the Gorge of the Redwall Limestone
Miles 25 to 27

opposite page right:

At Mile 26.5, a group plays Hacky Sack at camp in the gorge.

Entering the Gorge of the Redwall Limestone (cont.)
Miles 25 to 27

left:

Cave Springs Rapid, at Mile 25.3, ends the Roaring Twenties. It has a drop of 6 feet and is rated 5.

right:

For some distance along the left side of Mile 27, the limestone is fantastically fluted and polished, as seen here. The sculpting and polishing of rocks at riverside is not the work of the water directly, but of the abrasive materials transported by the river. As silt-laden water swirls in eddies along the banks, these abrasives are whirled in circular currents against rock surfaces, both sculpting and polishing the rocks.

Major John Wesley Powell, the first person to run the Grand Canyon, said of the Redwall Limestone: "The limestone of this canyon is often polished and makes a beautiful marble." It was on the basis of this statement that this portion of the Grand Canyon has come to be called Marble Canyon.

Marble Canyon

Miles 28-61

The latter portion of Marble Canyon is known more for its scenic attributes than its rapids. The great cliff of the Redwall Limestone dominates this stretch. Side canyons in the Redwall and the underlying Muav Limestone are numerous and appealing, especially Silver Grotto in Shinumo Wash and Buck Farm and Saddle canyons. Other unique features include the waterfalls and flower gardens of Vaseys Paradise, Redwall Cavern, the fossils at Nautiloid Canyon, Royal Arches, President Harding Rapid, and the Indian ruins at Nankoweap Creek.

In its final 10 miles, Marble Canyon widens as it runs through the soft Bright Angel Shale. Just above the confluence of the Little Colorado River, river runners encounter for the first time the Tapeats Sandstone, the lowermost of the horizontal sedimentary layers that account for the characteristic stair-step look of the Grand Canyon.

Marble Canyon ends where the Little Colorado River joins the Colorado, running either an unexpected turquoise blue or mud red.

opposite page:
Recreation in Redwall Cavern, Mile 33

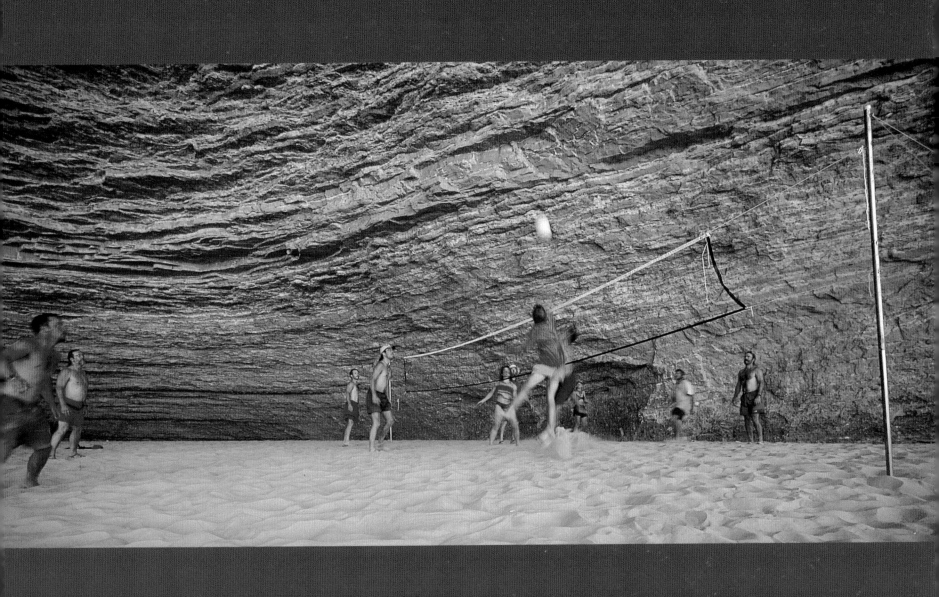

Silver Grotto
Mile 29

above:

The sedimentary layers in the Redwall are exposed to view, across from the raft pulling in to Silver Grotto. High water has removed the red stain (derived from the Hermit Formation), revealing the underlying structure of the rock.

right:

In cool weather, Silver Grotto is known as Shiver Grotto because, to progress farther, one must swim this first pool.

far right:

The uppermost pool

opposite page left:

The oval pool has a short, steep, curving wall at its head. With sufficient speed it's possible to run right around the head of the pool, adhering to the steeply banked wall by virtue of centrifugal force. If you fail, you fall in.

Mile 30

opposite page right:

Calm waters reflect the Redwall. The head of 30 Mile Rapid (unrated) is seen downstream.

South Canyon
Mile 31.6

above right:

The Redwall across the river is framed by the mouth of South Canyon.

below left:

South Canyon is home to a group of ring-tails. This nocturnal animal will tear into any food or garbage left out.

below center:

Vaseys Paradise can be seen downstream from camp at South Canyon, where an early breakfast is being prepared.

below right:

A Supai boulder wedged into the narrow bed of South Canyon is one of many chock-stones that make the walk up the canyon a rock-climbing exercise.

Vaseys Paradise
Mile 31.9

above:

Vaseys Paradise was named by Powell for a biologist friend. The Redwall is honey-combed by cave systems, some of which contain streams that drain from the plateaus high above. Vaseys is one of a number of streams that pour from cave mouths in the Redwall.

right:

A dory approaches Vaseys Paradise. Stantons Cave is seen in the cliff behind.

far right:

The fluted surface of a riverside limestone boulder at Vaseys Paradise

Vaseys Paradise (cont.)
Mile 31.9

left:

Yellow monkeyflower

above:

Red monkeyflower

opposite page above left:

Poison ivy and cardinal flowers grow in the moist surroundings of the stream at Vaseys.

opposite page below left:

Orchids

Redwall Cavern
Mile 33

opposite page right:

Sacred datura decorates the beach to the side of Redwall Cavern.

Redwall Cavern (cont.)

Mile 33

above:

Redwall Cavern is a deep recess, which Powell estimated to be large enough to accommodate 50,000 people. It's a cool and restful place.

Mile 34

opposite page:

This is my favorite view, but unlike other such aisles, it hasn't been named. The Muav Limestone appears at the base of the Redwall cliff.

Nautiloid Canyon
Mile 34.8

left:

Pool at the mouth of Nautiloid Canyon. After a short scramble from the mouth, fossil nautiloids can be found in the limestone bedrock of Nautiloid Canyon.

below:

A nautiloid is an extinct cephalopod. The fossil in the photo has been splashed with water to bring out the detail.

Tatahatso Wash to Buck Farm Canyon
Miles 37.4 to 41

opposite page left:

Buck Farm Canyon, at Mile 41, has a slot portion cut into the Muav Limestone.

opposite page above right:

Channel fill at Mile 38. Seen here at the contact between the Redwall Limestone and the underlying Muav Limestone, a river channel on the surface of the Muav was filled by the marine deposits of the Temple Butte Limestone. In this area of the Canyon, the Temple Butte was subsequently eroded completely away, except for where it filled this and other channels. In the western end of the Canyon, a thin Temple Butte layer merges into the base of the Redwall cliff.

opposite page below center:

This portion of Marble Canyon has good rainbow trout fishing. (Photo by Kathy Miller)

opposite page right:

Camp at the bend below Tatahatso Wash at Mile 37.7

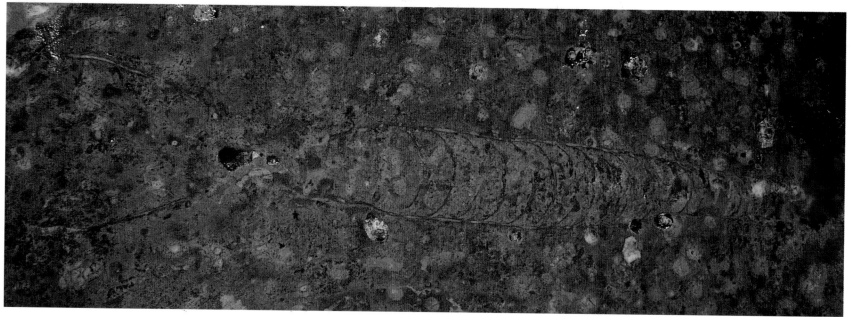

Approaching President Harding Rapid
Mile 42

left:

The approach to President Harding Rapid passes along the sunlit north wall of Point Hansbrough.

right:

A mule deer buck. Deer frequent the wooded shoreline in this area.

below right:

The Royal Arches are located on a bend to the left at Mile 41.5.

President Harding Rapid
Mile 43.7

opposite page:

President Harding Rapid sits at the foot of Point Hansbrough. The photo was taken from the Eminence Break Trail, which begins at the Mile 44.6 camp, on river left below President Harding Rapid. The Eminence Break is a fault that cuts through the rim of the Canyon, providing a route into and out of the Canyon. President Harding Rapid consists of one immense midstream boulder. It drops 4 feet and is rated 2-4.

Saddle Canyon

Mile 47

opposite page left:

Across from the upper camp at Saddle Canyon, the canyon wall glows with reflected light.

opposite page center:

A trail leads into Saddle Canyon, which narrows ahead.

opposite page right:

A waterfall ends the slot portion of Saddle Canyon, which is cut into the Muav Limestone.

Mile 50

right:

This downstream view shows the brightly lit Redwall and Muav cliff. The slope-forming Bright Angel Shale is at river level.

Nankoweap Creek
Mile 52

opposite page:

Looking upstream over Nankoweap Delta, this rim-to-river view is taken from the base of the Redwall cliff, at the "granaries"—food storage structures built under an overhang by the aboriginal inhabitants of the Grand Canyon. These native Americans were once known as the Anasazi, which is a Navajo word for "ancient enemies." Archeologists have renamed them the "ancestral Puebloan people." Nankoweap Rapid (seen here) is long but inconsequential. It drops 25 feet and is rated 3.

right:

The downstream view from the granaries

Kwagunt Rapid
Mile 56

below:

A raft enters Kwagunt Rapid on the left tongue, to the left of a very large hole. Kwagunt Rapid has a drop of 7 feet and is rated 4-6. It is scouted from the left.

Awatubi Canyon

Mile 58.3

opposite page:

Awatubi Canyon, on river right, faces the Desert Façade, a rim-to-river cliff. In this upstream view, stormy evening light illuminates the uppermost cliff.

The Little Colorado River

Mile 61.4

right:

The Little Colorado River is the largest tributary to the Colorado in the Grand Canyon, and it has carved a magnificent canyon of its own. Here, a yellow wall of the Muav stands in the foreground, with the Redwall behind.

The Little Colorado River (cont.)
Mile 61.4

left:

When the Little Colorado is not carrying runoff, it is a turquoise blue, a color derived from mineral-laden springs upstream in its canyon. When it is carrying runoff, it is a ruddy red-brown and discolors the Colorado. Here, the turquoise waters of the Little Colorado mix with the green water of the Colorado.

right:

A travertine dam in the Little Colorado River

opposite page:

An oar trip lunches at the mouth of the Little Colorado.

MILES 28-61

The Little Colorado River (cont.)

Mile 61.4

opposite page:

Upstream view in the canyon of the Little Colorado River

above left:

The mouth of the Little Colorado is one of the "attraction spots" (as characterized by the Park Service) that typically gets congested with visitors. Here, rafts and dories crowd in.

above center:

Bobcat tracks in salt-encrusted mud in the bed of the Little Colorado

above right:

Swimming in the warm Little Colorado

below left:

Boulders in the Little Colorado

below right:

Fluted limestone boulder in the Little Colorado

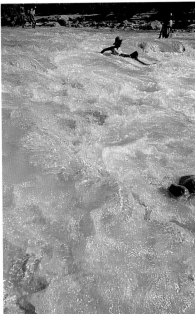

CH **3**

To the
Upper
Granite
Gorge
Miles 62–77

A short gorge of the hard Tapeats Sandstone begins immediately below the Little Colorado, followed by the first appearance of the Grand Canyon Supergroup assemblage of rocks. These are Precambrian sedimentary rocks that, as a group, have been dramatically tilted by long-ago tectonic activity.

The Canyon widens again as the Colorado River cuts through the first member of the group, the soft Dox Sandstone. The canyon only narrows 10 miles downstream with the first appearance of the harder Shinumo Quartzite. The much-visited South Rim of the Grand Canyon comes into sight downstream.

Tanner Canyon, Unkar Creek, and Hance rapids provide escalating whitewater challenges. In particular, Hance Rapid, the last feature of this section, is the hardest yet negotiated.

opposite:
Turned around in Unkar Rapid at **Mile 72.5**

The Gorge of the Tapeats Sandstone and Carbon Creek

Miles 62 to 64.6

opposite page above left:

The tarp is tied off to an arm of rock at camp in the Tapeats gorge at Mile 62.5. The gorge, which extends from the confluence of the Little Colorado downstream to Mile 65, is formed of the ledgy Tapeats Sandstone.

opposite page below left:

At Mile 64, an oar raft drifts past salt seeps in the Tapeats.

opposite page right:

The Palisades of the Desert, seen from Carbon Creek at Mile 64.6, is a rim-to-river cliff that towers steeply overhead.

below and right:

In early spring, clear water in Carbon Creek flows over the colorful Bright Angel Shale.

The Gorge of the Tapeats Sandstone and Carbon Creek (cont.)
Miles 62 to 64.6

above:

In Carbon Creek, the Butte Fault has bent the normally horizontal ledges of the Tapeats skyward.

Lava Canyon Rapid, Palisades Creek, and Comanche Point
Miles 65.5 to 68

opposite page:

The Canyon widens dramatically at Lava Canyon Rapid (Mile 65.5), as it cuts through the soft Dox Sandstone. Canyons of hard rock are steeply walled, whereas soft rocks erode into wide valleys. The South Rim comes into view downstream. Lava Canyon Rapid has a drop of 4 feet and is rated 2-4.

MILES 62-77

Lava Canyon Rapid, Palisades Creek, and Comanche Point (cont.)
Miles 65.5 to 68

far left:

Comanche Point, at Mile 67, is a prominent landmark on river left.

left:

Palisades Creek is located on the left at Lava Canyon Rapid. The tilted reddish Dox Sandstone, which appears in the vicinity of Palisades Creek, is seen at the bottom of the photo. The Dox, which was formed in the Precambrian Era more than 1090 million years ago, is the oldest layer yet to appear.

The Dox is a member of the Grand Canyon Supergroup series of rocks, which appear here for the first time and again in a few places downstream. This group of rocks has been tilted, while the rocks above have preserved their original flat sedimentary planes. These rocks appear only in areas where faulting displaced them downward and saved them from erosion, which removed them elsewhere.

Besides the Dox, the Grand Canyon Supergroup includes the Shinumo Quartzite, the Hakatai Shale, and the Bass Limestone, which will all be encountered downstream, right to the beginning of the Upper Granite Gorge at Mile 77.

Tanner Canyon Rapid to Cardenas Creek
Miles 68.5 to 71

above:

Tanner Canyon Rapid drops 20 feet and is rated 2-4, but it has one wave that can flip a boat.

below:

Below Tanner, the river meanders through the broad and open Dox valley to Cardenas Creek, on river left. Vishnu Temple, a major inner canyon feature, is seen on the skyline.

opposite page:

Apollo Temple, a monument of Redwall Limestone, appears on the skyline across from the mouth of Cardenas Creek, as boats are loaded in the morning. The black Basalt Cliffs lie beneath the cliff of Tapeats Sandstone and overlie the Dox Sandstone. From the camp at Cardenas Creek, a trail leads downstream to a vantage point overlooking Unkar Creek Rapid.

Tanner Canyon Rapid to Cardenas Creek (cont.)
Miles 68.5 to 71

left:

A rainstorm at Cardenas Creek produces a visual effect common to mountains and canyons, as the rain increasingly veils the more distant ridges. Escalante Butte, at the head of Cardenas Creek, rises on photo left.

Unkar Creek Rapid Overlook
Above Mile 72.5

right:

Illuminated by the setting sun, the South Rim is seen in the photo of lower Unkar Creek Rapid.

Mile 73.5

left:

At Mile 73.5, on river right, a rib of Dox Sandstone projects into the river, creating a turbulent eddy below it. The flutings seen here are the work of the fast-moving water (and the sand it carries) in that eddy.

Mile 74 Camp

right:

View upstream at Mile 74 camp. From this camp, a trail leads up a long ridge to the west, and ends at a monument known as the Tabernacle. From there, one can hike to a dramatic overlook just downstream of Hance Rapid, above Mile 77.

Hance Rapid Overlook
Above Mile 77

above left:

From Hance Rapid overlook, 1600 feet above the river, the rapid is seen just upstream. Across from the mouth of Red Canyon, the cliff is Shinumo Quartzite, which overlies the Hakatai Shale.

below left:

The downstream view shows a riffle at the mouth of Mineral Canyon and the beginning of the Upper Granite Gorge. Also seen in this view are the white tailings of the old Hance asbestos mine. The reddish slope is the Hakatai Shale.

75 Mile Creek

opposite page left:

On river left, the slot canyon of 75 Mile Creek is cut into the Shinumo Quartzite, which first appears here.

Hance Rapid
Mile 76.7

opposite page right:

Hance Rapid is long and complicated, with any number of possible runs. The boat in the photo is seen halfway through the rapid, which drops 30 feet and is rated 8-10. The nature of the difficulties in this rapid is largely dependent on water level. The slope behind the boat is Hakatai Shale, overlain by a cliff of Shinumo Quartzite.

The
Upper
Granite
Gorge
Miles 78-98

Hance Rapid is still in sight when you enter the Inner Gorge of the Grand Canyon, beginning here with the Upper Granite Gorge. From river level, the entire aspect of the Canyon changes, from brightly colored stratified rocks to somber-hued metamorphic rocks. Steep and jagged ridges, gullies, and crags now predominate.

Sockdolager Rapid awaits, less than 2 miles downstream. It is the first of a series of very difficult rapids that ends with Crystal Rapid 20 miles downstream.

Respite comes in the form of stops at Clear Creek and Bright Angel Creek. At the latter you'll even find a little bit of civilization at Phantom Ranch. Some river travelers may leave the river at Phantom Ranch to hike or ride a mule out of the Canyon, while others will do the reverse, taking their places. For the newcomers, the sore knees and sweat and dust of the trail are immediately put out of mind by the crashing holes of Horn Creek Rapid, just downstream at Mile 90.

Soon thereafter, in quick succession, come Granite and Hermit rapids (miles 93 and 94). The former is known for its large, crisscrossing waves, and the latter is famous for its series of five haystack waves, each larger than the one that precedes it.

The intimidating Crystal Rapid is the climactic conclusion to this first portion of the Upper Granite Gorge. Things mellow out downstream.

opposite:
Seen from camp at the head of Crystal Rapid, at Mile 98.2, this downstream telephoto view is of sunrise gilding Scorpion Ridge, against a stormy sky.

Entering the Upper Granite Gorge
Miles 77 and 78

opposite page:

The Upper Granite Gorge begins immediately below Hance Rapid, at Mile 77. But "Granite Gorge" is a misnomer. The rock most widely represented in the three Granite Gorges is Vishnu Schist. (Along with other metamorphic rocks, this complex is now referred to as the Vishnu basement rocks, but for brevity, I will continue to refer to them as Vishnu Schist or just the Vishnu.) Igneous (molten) rocks such as the Zoroaster Granite have been intruded into the metamorphic rocks. The pinkish veins of the Zoroaster Granite appear shortly downstream. The Grand Canyon Supergroup of tilted Precambrian rocks that has been at riverside since approximately Mile 64 will soon pinch out, between the Tapeats Sandstone above and the Vishnu Schist below.

The contact between the Tapeats and the underlying Vishnu is known as the Great Unconformity, a reference to the great amount of time missing here from the geologic record. The polished and fluted Vishnu Schist, gray colored in this photo and seen close to the boats, first appears here and will rise rapidly in height as the Supergroup disappears. The Vishnu Schist takes on many colors, depending on its source rock—the particular type of rock, sedimentary or igneous, that metamorphosed into schist as the result of heat and pressure being applied to the rocks by earth (tectonic) movements. The different colored schists have, in the past, been given individual names, including the Brahma and Rama.

above:

This upstream view, at Mile 78, shows the sequence of rocks from the uppermost cliff of pink Shinumo Quartzite, down through a slope of reddish Hakatai Shale, a cliff of reddish Bass Limestone, and a black diabase sill (diabase is an intrusive rock), to the rising walls of the Vishnu Schist.

The Vishnu Schist
Miles 78 to 84

above:

Black schist near Clear Creek at Mile 84

right:

Brown schist at Mile 78

far right:

Exotically sculpted black schist encountered while scouting Grapevine Rapid at Mile 81.5

Sockdolager and Grapevine Rapids
Miles 78.6 and 81.5

above left:

Coming soon after Hance Rapid, Sockdolager Rapid, a.k.a. "Sock," is challenging, especially if you run the central "sockdolager" waves (in Powell's day, sockdolager meant a knock-out punch). Two big, oblique waves form a V, and you need to be facing the one you hit, unless you run straight ahead, aiming for the apex of the V. On one occasion, I had decided to run the right wave, so I faced right as I pushed the boat rightward. But I didn't get there.

Consequently, I rode up sideways on the left wave and was rolled over. In the photo, the raft hits the V straight on and remains right-side up, albeit full of water.

above right:

Depending on the river's water level, boaters may be able to sneak to the left, which the open canoe succeeds at doing. Sockdolager has a drop of 19 feet and is rated 8-9.

below left:

Grapevine Rapid is easier than Sockdolager and is usually run right down the middle, as seen here. It drops 17 feet and is rated 6-8.

Mile 82

opposite page:

In this upstream view below Grapevine Rapid, pink granite dikes rise vertically along river right. The South Rim is on the far horizon.

Clear Creek

Mile 84

above:

Clear Creek is a perennial stream with wonderful rock formations at and near its mouth, such as these rock ribs.

MILES 78-98

Chapter 4: The Upper Granite Gorge

Clear Creek (cont.)
Mile 84

opposite page left:

An evening downstream telephoto view from the mouth of Clear Creek

opposite page right:

Along the creek, the schist is silvery and gleams in the sun.

below left:

The beach at Clear Creek camp, located about a hundred yards upstream of the mouth

Below Clear Creek
Miles 84 to 87

right:

In the vicinity of Mile 85, a promontory of Tapeats juts out over soaring ribs of granite and schist.

Below Clear Creek (cont.)
Miles 84 to 87

opposite page:

At Mile 86, a downstream view of the chaotic formations of schist and granite in the Upper Granite Gorge

above:

Cremation Camp, at Mile 87, is just upstream from Bright Angel Creek. It is used by trips that will be doing exchanges—dropping some people off and receiving others. The proximity of this camp to the trail system at Bright Angel Creek allows hikers to get an early start for the 9-mile climb out of the canyon.

Bright Angel Creek
Mile 87.5

right:

Bright Angel Creek is the location of Phantom Ranch, along with a ranger station, a campground, and two bridges that service the cross-canyon trail system. Phantom Ranch is named for Phantom Creek, which joins Bright Angel Creek just upstream of the ranch. River runners can buy cold drinks and send and receive mail at Phantom Ranch!

Bright Angel Creek (cont.)
Mile 87.5

left:

Kaibab Bridge and the beach at the up-stream end of the Bright Angel Creek delta (Photo by David Hiser)

Horn Creek Rapid
Mile 90.2

opposite page above:

Horn Creek Rapid is rough … and it is the initiation for those river runners who join trips at Bright Angel Creek. Here, a group of kayakers run the big waves, right down the middle. Horn Creek has a drop of 10 feet and is rated 7-10.

Trinity Creek
Mile 91.5

right:

The slot canyon of Trinity Creek is a short walk up from the small beach at its mouth.

Granite Rapid
Mile 93.4

opposite page below:

The excitement continues through this portion of the canyon. The run along the wall in Granite Rapid is a thriller. Huge waves carom off the wall and collide with waves breaking from the other direction, making a maelstrom of whitewater that quickly takes over. One such wave is seen here.

Hermit Rapid, Wave #5

Mile 95

opposite page above left:

Right after Granite comes Hermit Rapid, which, at levels in excess of 15,000 cfs, gets my vote as the most memorable rapid in the Grand Canyon. The entry is on the tongue. There follows a sequence of five perfectly shaped pyramidal waves, each bigger than the one that preceded it. After climbing to the crest of wave #4, wave #5 appears as a mountain of water, separated from your position atop #4 by a deep valley. Dropping into and climbing out of that trough can take three full seconds. Then comes the crest of #5: Will you make it through? In this photo, Bill and Bernadette Gould go right over the top.

opposite page above right:

Joel Blitstein is submerged on the way through.

opposite page below left:

In this photo, my stepdaughter, Laina, the sole occupant of the boat, "high-sides" (moves to the high side of the boat in the attempt to prevent a flip) by throwing her weight to the bow to keep it down. She is lost to view in the wave crashing down upon her.

opposite page center right:

Molly and Maria get turned sideways and are in danger of sliding back down the face of the wave. But they too made it through. Hermit has a drop of 15 feet and is rated 8-9.

opposite page below right:

Seen from the opposite side of the river, the author tops wave #4 and has #5 squarely in his sights. (Photo by Kathy Miller)

Mile 96 Camp to Mile 97

above:

On river left, this is a beautiful camp with an upstream view of the Great Mohave Wall on the South Rim, seen here.

Mile 96 Camp to Mile 97 (cont.)

left:

This downstream view, at Mile 98.2, is of the placid approach to Crystal Rapid.

Crystal Rapid
Mile 98.2

opposite page above left:

Crystal Rapid was transformed from innocuous to one of the two hardest rapids in the Grand Canyon by a massive debris flow in the winter of 1966. Crystal flipped a 19-foot pontoon boat I was riding on my first trip in 1971. The high water of 1983, when Lake Powell almost overtopped Glen Canyon Dam, changed it for the harder. It stayed that way until 1996, when an intentional flood release changed it for the easier. The 1995 right run shown in this sequence starts here with the oarswoman, Molly, rowing hard downstream and to the right, while looking over her shoulder at the huge top hole that must be avoided.

opposite page above right:

Molly passes just to the right of the hole.

opposite page below:

Molly passes to the right of the second hole, which effectively ends the right run. Crystal Rapid drops 17 feet and is rated a 10.

CH **5**

The
Upper and Middle
Granite Gorges
Miles 99-130

Downstream of Crystal Rapid is a section of the Upper Granite Gorge called the Gems (miles 100 to 107), named for side canyons that include Agate, Turquoise, Ruby, and Sapphire. The name is appropriate: The abundance of lighter-colored crystalline rock makes the Gems a bright and sparkly place. While there are many rapids in the Gems, they are less challenging than those found immediately upstream.

The Gems end at Bass Rapid, at the entry to the Shinumo Amphitheater. A popular hike follows Shinumo Creek and its tributary, White Creek, upstream, along the old North Bass Trail.

Walthenberg Rapid (Mile 112) precedes the multitiered Elves Chasm, the most exquisite of all the side canyons. The Upper Granite Gorge ends just downstream of Elves Chasm, as the river re-enters the Tapeats Sandstone. Several moderate rapids occur in this 10-mile stretch, which ends with the reappearance of metamorphic rock and the beginning of the short (but sensational) Middle Granite Gorge at Mile 127. The difficult Specter and Bedrock rapids conclude the Middle Granite Gorge.

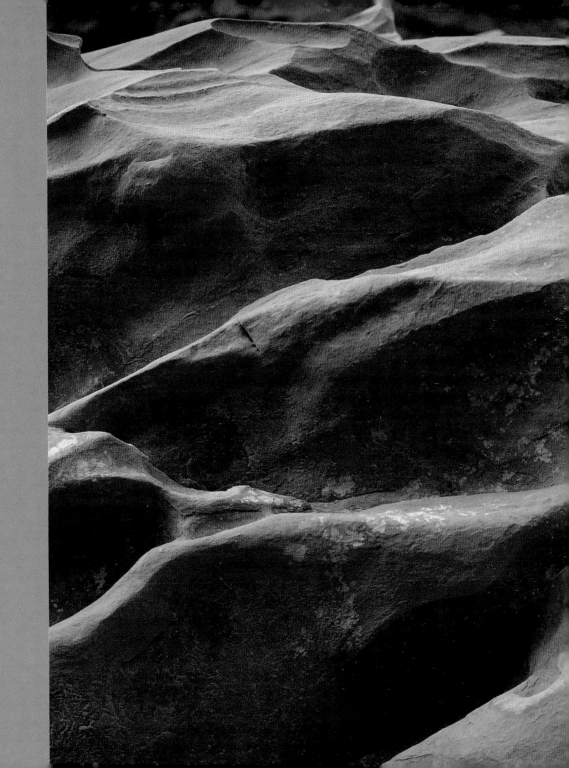

Sculpted sandstone boulder at
Specter Rapid, Mile 129

MILES 99-130

Tuna Creek Rapid

Mile 99.3

opposite page left:

As you approach Tuna Creek Rapid, you are still relishing having learned your ABCs—Alive Below Crystal. The photo shows a wall of silvery schist seamed by dikes of pink granite.

opposite page above right:

An upstream view from in the rapid. Tuna Creek Rapid has a drop of 10 feet and is rated 5-7.

The Gems

Miles 100 to 107

opposite page below right:

Polished black schist on river left

above:

Sculpted tan schist on river left

The Gems (cont.)
Miles 100 to 107

left:

Polished black schist on river right,
upstream of 104 Mile Rapid

right:

A hole in granite

Turquoise, Ruby, and Bass Rapids

Miles 102 to 107

above:

Bass Rapid, at Mile 107.8, has a drop of 5 feet and is rated 4-6. The Shinumo Amphitheater opens up downstream of Bass Rapid, in this view to the North Rim. Again, as a result of faulting, this area has exposures of the Grand Canyon Supergroup, which includes the Shinumo Quartzite.

below far left:

Ruby Rapid, at Mile 104.5, describes a long curve to the left. More than halfway down is a hole that can flip a boat. Ruby has a drop of 11 feet and is rated 4-7.

below left:

At Mile 102, a paddle raft approaches Turquoise Rapid, which has a drop of 4 feet and is rated 4-6.

Bass Camp and Shinumo Creek
Mile 108.5

opposite page left:

The choice Bass Camp campsite, on river right a short distance upstream from the mouth of Shinumo Creek, is where the North Bass Trail departs for the North Rim via Shinumo and White creeks.

opposite page right:

From the trail, as it descends to Shinumo Creek

left:

In Redwall Canyon, a side canyon of White Creek, a large chockstone is wedged into the Tapeats Sandstone.

right:

Blooming Utah agave seen along the trail to Shinumo Creek

Bass Camp Shoreline

far left:

The shoreline immediately upstream of Bass Camp has some of the most fantastically sculpted rocks to be seen in the Canyon, including this fluted black schist rock surrounded by lighter schist.

left:

At riverside, a highly eroded spur of black schist and quartz

Hakatai Rapid
Miles 110 to 111

right:

Hakatai Rapid, at Mile 110.7, has a drop of 8 feet and is rated 4-5. (Photo by Kathy Miller)

left:

Silvery schist and pink granite

Walthenberg Rapid
Mile 112.2

In the photo, a barely visible kayaker is
about to plunge into the one very large hole
in Walthenberg Rapid, which has a drop of
14 feet and is rated 6-9.

Mile 114

far left:

This upstream view shows Wheeler Point, on the North Rim, above the sunlit Redwall. The Upper Granite Gorge is decreasing in depth (soon to end) and, thus, the Tapeats is coming closer overhead.

left:

Buttress of Redwall opposite Mile 114 camp. Elves Chasm is coming up!

Elves Chasm

Mile 116.6

opposite page:

Elves Chasm is the most enchanting side canyon in the Grand Canyon, with a succession of tiers and waterfalls that ascend to a final amphitheater. Caution, however, is urged for those attempting the climb. Some rock climbing is required, and a rope and anchors are useful in safeguarding some of the more difficult and exposed moves. As with all Grand Canyon dayhikes, be sure to take a first-aid kit.

At the mouth of Elves Chasm, travertine boulders sit atop pink granite bedrock. The cliff in the background is the Tapeats Sandstone.

right:

The first fall is perhaps the best of several in Elves Chasm. Maidenhair fern clings to the rock.

Elves Chasm (cont.)
Mile 116.6

left:
Red monkeyflower and maidenhair fern grow beside the creek as it flows over pink granite at the mouth of Elves Chasm.

right:
Rushes arch over the creek near the mouth.

opposite page:
An algae-choked pool reflects the sky and clouds.

Elves Chasm (cont.)
Mile 116.6

far left:

Yellow columbine grows in the spray of waterfalls.

above left:

Travertine boulders line a pool near the final amphitheater in Elves Chasm.

below left:

Cardinal flowers grow on the uppermost level of Elves Chasm.

opposite page left:

Descending ledges—one of the few sunny spots in Elves Chasm

opposite page right:

A detail of travertine deposition

MILES 99-130

Blacktail Canyon
Miles 120 and 121

opposite page:

The Upper Granite Gorge ends shortly below Elves Chasm. Here, in Conquistador Aisle, at Mile 121, the river runs through the Tapeats.

left:

Moonrise at Blacktail Camp, at Mile 120

Forster and Fossil Rapids
Miles 122.8 to 125

above right:

The long Fossil Rapid, at Mile 125, runs through the Tapeats. It has a drop of 15 feet and is rated 6-7.

below right:

Forster Rapid, at Mile 122.8, also runs through the Tapeats. It has a drop of 7 feet and is rated a 6.

Randy's Rock Camp and the Middle Granite Gorge

Miles 126.3 to 130.5

left:

The spacious and scenic camp at Mile 126.3 is known to guides and river runners as Randy's Rock Camp. Randy's Rock is a massive hunk of Tapeats that has fallen into the river, but it is easy to miss—unless, of course, you are asleep. As the story goes, a boatman by the name of Randy did just that. He hit the rock and flipped his boat. The Middle Granite Gorge begins just downstream with the reappearance of schist and associated rocks.

right:

Barrel cacti dot a slope of schist, with the Tapeats close overhead.

opposite page left:

In the late afternoon, the Redwall glows pink.

opposite page right:

Telephoto view to the South Rim, showing the schist, the Supai, and the Kaibab Rimrock.

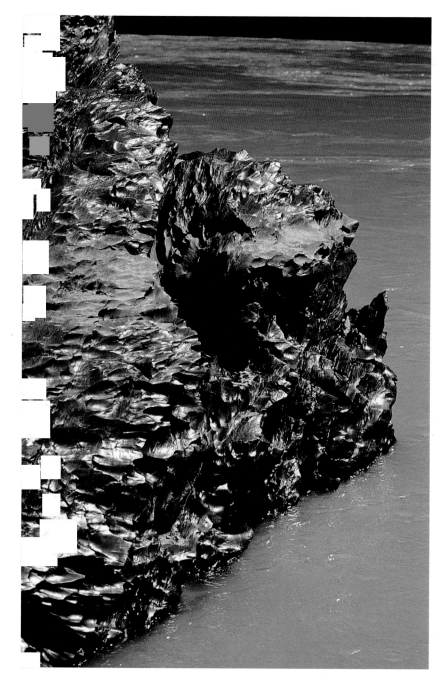

Randy's Rock Camp and the Middle Granite Gorge (cont.)
Miles 126.3 to 130.5

opposite page left:

Fluted black schist

opposite page above right:

Polished black schist and orange granite

opposite page below right:

Salt pendants

Specter and Bedrock Rapids
Miles 129 to 130.5

above right:

Specter Rapid was once rated 3, but it has become considerably more difficult over time, again as a result of debris flows narrowing the channel. The raft shown here flipped immediately after the photo was taken. Specter Rapid has a drop of 6 feet and is rated 5-8.

below:

You have to row hard to the right to avoid running into the bedrock island in Bedrock Rapid, which has a drop of 8 feet and is rated an 8.

To Kanab Creek

Miles 131-143

Below Bedrock Rapid the river exits the Middle Granite Gorge and runs through a sill of dark diabase rock. This stretch of the Colorado contains one major rapid and three of the best side canyon stops in the entire river corridor.

Deubendorff Rapid, at Mile 131.8, precedes the large drainage system of Tapeats Creek and Thunder River. The hike up Tapeats Creek to Thunder River is one of the high points of running the Grand.

Metamorphic and igneous rock reappear downstream of Tapeats Creek, where the river squeezes through Granite Narrows. Next is Deer Creek Falls and the Deer Creek Gorge, at Mile 136, another not-to-be-missed stop. Some river runners hike from Tapeats to Deer Creek, while others take their boats down for them.

After Deer Creek, the river re-enters the Tapeats Sandstone and then the Muav Limestone. Kanab Creek, a major tributary that heads beyond the northern perimeter of the Grand Canyon, enters on the right. A scenic hike up Kanab Creek, which concludes this section of the river corridor, takes you to Whispering Falls.

opposite page:
Gymnastics at Deer Creek Gorge, Mile 136.3

Deubendorff Rapid
Mile 131.8

left:

A variety of rocks can be seen while scouting Deubendorff Rapid on river left, including this rock assemblage.

right:

Deubendorff Rapid is long and tricky. It drops 15 feet and is rated 7-9. At a forgiving level, the raft hits a breaking wave at the top of the rapid.

opposite page above left:

Rock and grass

opposite page below left:

Veneer on limestone boulder

opposite page right:

Rock and water

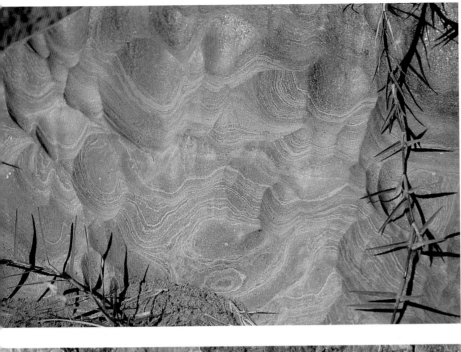

Tapeats Creek
Mile 133.8

left:

This downstream telephoto view was taken from the mouth of Tapeats Creek. On the left is the diabase; to the right is the Redwall and Muav. Like Bass Camp, Tapeats Creek is a favorite layover camp, which provides time for hiking upcanyon.

Tapeats Creek is one of a number of large northside streams. The larger streams come off the North Rim for two reasons: The North Rim is higher in elevation than the South Rim, and the Kaibab Plateau, which backs the North Rim, drains toward the Canyon. The South Rim, on the other hand, drains away from the Canyon. This is because the Colorado did not cut through the uplift at its highest point, but along its southern slope.

The larger volume of water in these north-side streams has caused them to erode their canyons farther back than typical south-side streams and has, thus, moved the North Rim farther back from the river corridor than is the South Rim.

above:

The mouth of Tapeats Creek and Tapeats Rapid, seen from the trail to upper Tapeats Creek. Tapeats Rapid drops 15 feet and is rated 4-5.

MILES 131-143

Tapeats Creek (cont.)
Mile 133.8
opposite page left:
The broad and scenic valley of upper Tapeats Creek, with cottonwood trees lining the stream

opposite page right:
Once again, the Grand Canyon Supergroup makes an appearance. A barrel cactus grows in the Hakatai Shale. Beyond it, the lower cliff is the purplish Shinumo Quartzite.

above:
Colorful Supergroup rocks are seen in the foreground; the Redwall is in the background.

below left:
The Grand Canyon rattlesnake in this photo shows the characteristic arrowhead-shaped pit viper head.

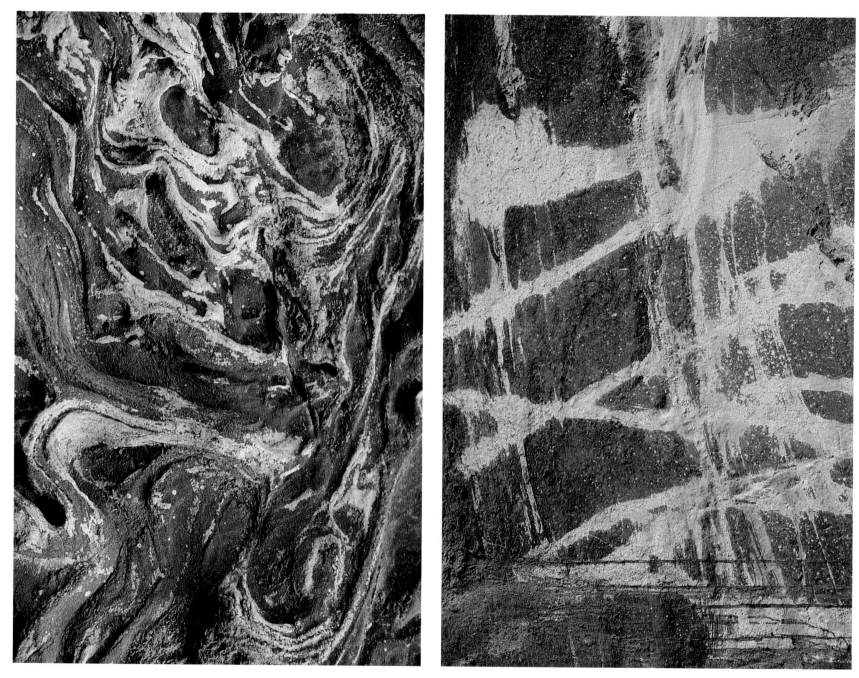

Red and White Place, Tapeats Creek

opposite page left:

No one knows for sure what happened to the Shinumo Quartzite to produce these fanciful designs in red and white, here seen as swirls.

opposite page right:

Here, seen as slashes

above:

A red and white cliff

MILES 131-143

Thunder River and Cave

opposite page left:

In June of a high water year, the aptly named Thunder River, a tributary to Tapeats Creek, crashes downhill from where it gushes out of its cave.

opposite page right:

The mouth of the main (left) opening of Thunder River cave is decorated with red monkeyflowers. In the fall, the volume of water that flows out of the cave is much reduced.

left:

A rainbow in the spray at the foot of the uppermost fall

right:

The uppermost fall

Granite Narrows
Mile 135
above:
Granite Narrows is the narrowest point
on the river, approximately 75 feet across.

Deer Creek Falls and Gorge
Mile 136.2
opposite page left:
Deer Creek Falls is situated within a
hundred yards of the river. Deer
Creek Gorge is cut in the Tapeats
Sandstone.

opposite page right:
From the ledge at the entrance to Deer
Creek Gorge is a view upstream to
Granite Narrows and beyond.

Deer Creek Falls and Gorge (cont.)
Mile 136.2

left:

From the foot of Deer Creek Falls, a trail leads up an adjacent hillside (beware of poison ivy) and enters Deer Creek Gorge on a broad shelf. The trail continues to the head of the gorge and the open valley above. In the vicinity of the "patio," a scenic resting spot at the head of the gorge, it's possible to climb down into the gorge and wade downstream until stopped by a waterfall. This is a view into the gorge from the trail. Seen by the creek below is a redbud tree that was later destroyed by a flood.

right:

In the gorge, the walls of Tapeats glow in reflected light.

opposite page left:

A waterfall at the head of the gorge, and the patio

opposite page right:

Screened by trees, the source of Deer Creek is, again, a cave. Watercress borders the pool in the foreground.

Fishtail Rapid to Kanab Creek
Miles 139 to 143.4

above:

Fishtail Rapid drops 10 feet and is rated 5-7.

opposite page left:

Canyon wall at Mile 143, with the Muav in the foreground and the Redwall in the background

opposite page above right:

A pinnacle of the yellowish Muav Limestone, with the Redwall beyond, at Mile 140

opposite page below right:

Boulders in Kanab Creek at Mile 143.4

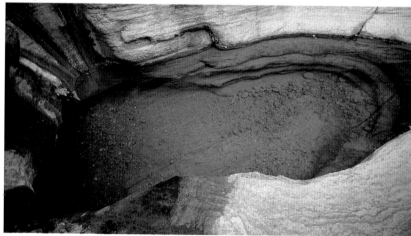

Fishtail Rapid to Kanab Creek (cont.)
Miles 139 to 143.4

above left:
Hikers in Kanab Creek

below left:
Pool in Kanab Creek

right:
The mouth of Kanab Creek

opposite page left:
Reflecting pool in Kanab Creek

opposite page right:
A few hours suffice for the hike to and from Whispering Falls.

The Gorge of the Muav Limestone

Miles 144-175

A long and confining gorge in the Muav Limestone is the site of numerous spectacular side canyons, which include Olo, Matkatamiba, Havasu, National, and Fern Glen canyons.

Entry to Olo is gained by climbing a rope. Matkatamiba was once used as the backdrop for a *Playboy* magazine spread—curves superimposed on curves! With its turquoise-tinted water, deep travertine pools, and waterfalls, Havasu Canyon is in a league by itself. Because camping is not permitted at the mouth, many trips camp both close upstream and close downstream of the mouth, so as to gain as many daylight hours at Havasu as possible.

The only rapid of consequence in this entire stretch is Upset Rapid, at Mile 149.7, which often does provide consequences. After Upset, river runners become preoccupied with Lava Falls Rapid, 29 miles downstream. Lava Falls is arguably the hardest rapid on the river.

Below Fern Glen, at Mile 168, the Canyon widens as the river re-enters the Bright Angel Shale and then the Tapeats. This section of the river corridor ends at Cove Canyon.

opposite page:
Water curl at Havasu Creek, Mile 156.6

MILES 144-175

Olo Canyon
Mile 145.5

opposite page left:

Olo Canyon, in the Muav Gorge, is a sensational slot canyon, but it requires you to climb a rope to gain admission.

opposite page right:

A slippery travertine cone is key to sur-mounting the second step in Olo.

left:

The stream and a pool, near the mouth

right:

Looking down the narrowest part of the slot canyon

Olo Canyon (cont.)
Mile 145.5

far left:
Looking back to the beach and the river

above:

**A short poem on the subject
of stranding:**

If you're running on high water

late in the day

this is the price you pay

for coming ashore

in a shallow bay.

On the beach at Olo

waiting to go.

left:
Pool

opposite page left:
Groove and pool

opposite page right:
Bedrock pool

Olo Canyon (cont.)
Mile 145.5

left:

Looking up the narrowest part of the slot canyon

right:

Pool in scalloped bedrock

opposite page above:

Mud curlicues

opposite page below:

Mud play at the mouth of Olo Canyon

Matkatamiba Canyon
Mile 147.9

left:

Not far downstream from Olo, Matkatamiba Canyon is another delight.

Nicknamed Matkat, it requires no effort to visit. The slot portion begins yards from the river. Beyond it, a broad amphitheater opens up, all within a quarter mile of the river.

Here, a chockstone of Supai Sandstone is wedged into the walls of Muav Limestone.

right:

Ferns and flowers

opposite page left:

A short waterfall is found at the entrance to the very narrow slot.

opposite page right:

A pool and grapevines beyond

Matkatamiba Canyon (cont.)

Mile 147.9

opposite page left:

Kathy Miller in the Matkat slot

opposite page right:

View toward the mouth

Upset Rapid to Mile 151.5 Camp

Miles 149.7 to 151.5

right:

A dory passes to the left of the huge central hole that gives Upset Rapid its name and reputation. Upset has a drop of 15 feet and is rated 6-9.

below:

Upset Rapid, the left run

**Upset Rapid to Mile 151.5
Camp (cont.)**
Miles 149.7 to 151.5

opposite page left:

The camp at Mile 151.5 is set into tiered Muav ledges. A delightful dripping spring and flower garden is found at the lower end of the camp.

Miles 155 and 156

opposite page right:

View downstream to the bend at Mile 155

above:

The Muav Gorge continues, with the "Mayan reliefs" (named for the resemblance to Mayan architecture), found in the vicinity of Mile 156. Havasu Creek is coming up!

The Mouth of Havasu Creek
Mile 156.6

left:

Havasu Creek is a world unto itself. At the mouth, the Colorado's flow determines the depth of the final pool in Havasu Creek, seen here.

right:

Rafts tie up to the overhanging walls. The color of Havasu Creek is by virtue of dissolved mineral salts—nice to look at, but not so good to drink.

opposite page:

The pool at the mouth

Along Lower Havasu Creek

left:

Wild grapes, known as Canyon grape

above right:

A young cottonwood tree

The Motor Pool, Havasu Creek

below right:

Relaxing at the motor pool

opposite page:

The so-called motor pool is an easy walk from the mouth, the destination for many of the guests of commercial motorized trips. Here, a huge chunk of travertine sits in the middle of the pool.

Beaver Falls, Havasu Creek

opposite page:

It's a good hike to Beaver Falls, taking most of the day for the round trip (not to mention time to enjoy the pools). Travertine dams have created deep pools and cascading waterfalls, seen here. Upstream from Beaver Falls are other waterfalls and the tiny town of Supai, all within the Havasupai Indian Reservation, which is best reached by foot, helicopter, or horseback from above.

left:

A travertine dam

right:

Trees bordering this pool at Beaver Falls have become partially submerged as the travertine dam has grown in height and deepened the pool.

Havasu Creek
Mile 156.6

opposite page left:

The warm colors of the canyon walls (especially in reflected light) and a turquoise creek—what a combination!

opposite page right:

Near the mouth, canyon walls glow with reflected light.

First Chance Camps
Miles 157.5 and 158.5

above left:

Camps at Miles 157.5 and 158.5 are known as the First Chance Camps. They provide the first chance to camp after a late departure from Havasu. Here are the "facilities" at the Mile 157.5 camp.

below left:

Diagramming Lava Falls at Mile 158.5 camp. It's Lava Day! Lava Falls awaits, 21 miles downstream. This Arizona Raft Adventures trip will run Lava in late afternoon. In this photo, head guide Steve Haase uses a sand diagram to brief guests on how he expects the group to run Lava.

Tuckup Canyon
Miles 161 to 165

right:

View downstream, vicinity Mile 161

Tuckup Canyon (cont.)
Miles 161 to 165

left:
Tuckup Canyon is seen on photo left in this upstream view from camp at Mile 165.

National Canyon
Mile 166.5

right:
Walls in National Canyon

opposite page left:
Moonset at dawn, National Canyon camp

opposite page right:
The photogenic Muav slot canyon is a short walk from either of the two camps at the mouth of National Canyon. This pool must be waded to reach the upper slot canyon.

National Canyon (cont.)
Mile 166.5

opposite page:

In the upper portion of the slot

Fern Glen to Cove Canyon
Miles 168 to 175

above left:

A snout-rig—a large raft with tubes tapered at the front end—approaches another scenic side canyon, Fern Glen.

above right:

The short hike into Fern Glen leads to a spacious amphitheater. At the upper end of the amphitheater, the scant flow of the creek has created a travertine cone.

below left:

Masses of maidenhair fern grow along seeps in Fern Glen.

below right:

Driftwood lies artfully sorted on a beach just below Cove Canyon.

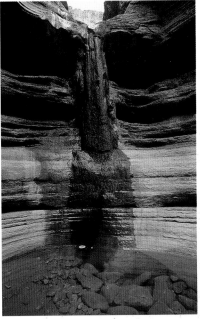

A Landscape
of
Lava

Miles 176-209

Vulcans Anvil, at Mile 178, announces the proximity both of the legendary Lava Falls Rapid and a landscape dominated by lava flows. The various flows, spread over many miles, are thought to be the best of their kind in the western United States. Here, river runners are treated to sights of lava rivers that cascaded down steep side canyons, of the remains of lava dams, of hunks of lava plastered to canyon walls, of huge lava boulders, and of the interesting and varied columnar jointing in the basalt rock.

At Whitmore Wash, at Mile 188, is a valley that was completely filled with lava. Near the riverside is a panel of red pictographs.

Continuing whitewater challenges are provided by 205 and 209 Mile rapids. The more serious of the two, 209 Mile Rapid, has an exploding wave/hole that flips many boats.

Granite Park, at Mile 209, sees the return of metamorphic and igneous rock.

opposite page:
Basalt cliff at Whitmore Trail, Mile 187.5

Vulcans Anvil to Lava Falls Rapid
Miles 178 and 179

left:

Lava, finally! Many river runners will have been consumed by a state of dread in the days leading up to Lava Falls. It is a serious rapid—no two ways about it. And it's the climax of running the Colorado River in the Grand Canyon.

Scouting Lava can be a long, drawn-out affair. One lingers on the shoreline, going over and over the intended line (the route through the rapid) and the moves that must be made to pull it off. Here, a river party is scouting the right run. The run starts on the tongue, in the lower left of the photo, and passes to the left of the huge crashing hole seen at the very bottom of the tongue (see page vi for a photo of a raft making this entry). Then the boat must be straightened out for the drop into the V-Wave, the white area across from the people on shore.

Once out of the V-Wave, the boat is full of water, and the last obstacles are the huge waves breaking just upstream of the Big Kahuna, the big black rock at top right in the photo.

Lava Falls, at Mile 179.3, drops 35 feet and is rated 10.

above right:

Scouting Lava from the left, as a motor rig dives into the right run

below right:

Vulcans Anvil, at Mile 178, is a volcanic plug—lava that solidified within a volcano. It sits in midstream, seen in this down-stream view from camp at Mile 177.8.

opposite page:

A self-bailing dory crashes through the biggest wave on the left run. This telephoto view compresses the river's width.

163

**Vulcans Anvil to
Lava Falls Rapid (cont.)**
Miles 178 and 179

opposite page:

The author in the V-Wave, on the right run. I'm leaning forward to avoid being knocked back and perhaps out of the boat. (Photo by Linde Waidhofer)

left:

Looking back upstream to Lava Falls. A broken-off hunk of basalt columns is seen in the foreground.

above right:

This raft started on the left run but ended up in the middle.

below left:

On the left run

below right:

Lava Falls is not a waterfall over a ledge of lava, as one might assume. Instead, it, like the great preponderance of rapids in the Grand Canyon, is the creation of debris flows, in this case coming out of Prospect Canyon, on river left. This canyon has a large drainage area and is sloped steeply down to the river, both factors that contribute to large floods and debris flows. Since I've been running the river, I've seen the delta at the mouth of the Prospect drainage enlarge and narrow the Colorado's channel by a full third. The raft seen in this photo is on the left run.

**Vulcans Anvil to
Lava Falls Rapid (cont.)**

Miles 178 and 179

left:

Just downstream of Lava, on the left, is Lava Spring. It's a perfect place to cool off and fill up.

The Lava Cascade

Miles 181 to 185

right:

Lava flows become commonplace in the Canyon for many miles downstream of Lava Falls. None is more dramatic than the one seen here, on the right at Mile 184, where lava cascaded steeply to the river from a volcano 3500 feet above.

opposite page:

View upstream toward Lava Falls, vicinity Mile 181

Basalt Columns
Miles 186 to 191

above left:

Basalt is the rock formed from lava flows in the Grand Canyon. These columns form as the lava slowly cools. The longer the lava took to cool, the larger they became. Because the lava cools more slowly at the bottom of the flow, the lowermost columns in a single flow will be larger than those that overlie them, as seen in this photo.

above center:

Vertical wall of columns

above right:

Overhanging wall of columns

Whitmore Wash
Mile 188

below right:

Pictographs, seen here at Whitmore Wash, are paintings on rock surfaces. (Petroglyphs are designs chipped into rock surfaces.)

opposite page:

Lava fills the Whitmore Valley.

Parashant Wash
Miles 193 to 198.5

opposite page left:

Teddybear cholla makes a rare appearance at Mile 193.

opposite page right:

Ocotillo is widespread in the lower Canyon. It blooms in the spring and leafs out after soaking rains.

left:

Parashant Wash, at Mile 198.5, is a major northside canyon. The group is returning from a visit to the "Book of Worms," a jumble of Bright Angel Shale with worm tracks found on the surfaces of individual slabs of rock.

205 Mile and 209 Mile Rapids
Miles 202 to 209

right:

205 Mile Rapid, a.k.a. Kolb Rapid, drops 17 feet and is rated 6-8.

205 Mile and 209 Mile Rapids (cont.)
Miles 202 to 209

opposite page:
In late afternoon, at Mile 202 camp, a pool on the shaded beach reflects the sunlit opposing canyon wall.

above:
At Granite Park and 209 Mile Rapid, near the beginning of the Lower Granite Gorge, granite and schist return. The big and broad exploding wave at 209 Mile Rapid is easily capable of flipping a boat if it explodes under you. Here, kayaker Brahm Reynolds successfully runs the hole.

The Lower. Granite Gorge

Miles 210-236

Once you're safely below the hole at 209 Mile Rapid, it's time to be on the lookout for the extraordinarily sculpted diorite at Mile 212, on river right. This is quickly followed, on river left, by sculpted Tapeats Sandstone, one of the few (if not only) such examples in the Canyon. Just yards downstream is the unique Pumpkin Springs.

The river flows in the Tapeats to Mile 215, where it enters Precambrian granite at the head of the Lower Granite Gorge. Providing the last big waves of the trip, 217 Mile Rapid gallops along a wall of light gray granite.

The Canyon widens at Mile 221. Diamond Peak appears downstream. At the base of Diamond Peak, the river enters a narrow granite gorge, which continues to Diamond Creek and beyond. Diamond Creek is the takeout for most river trips—only 10 miles upstream from where Lake Mead has buried the final 40 miles of the Colorado River in the Grand Canyon under lake water or exposed sediment.

Recently, sustained drought conditions have shrunk Lake Mead by half. The Colorado River now flows past the Grand Wash Cliffs, at Mile 277, and exits the Grand Canyon, cutting a new channel through collapsing beds of sediment.

At one time, Lake Mead extended upriver as far as Mile 236, and the photographic coverage of this book ends there.

opposite page:
Rafts tie up at Mile 212.

MILES 210-236

The Diorite at Mile 212
Miles 211 and 212
opposite page left:
Downstream view at Mile 211

opposite page right:
On river right, this small outcrop of Precambrian diorite is, in my opinion, the most gloriously sculpted rock in the Grand Canyon.

above:
A sculpted and polished bowl in the diorite

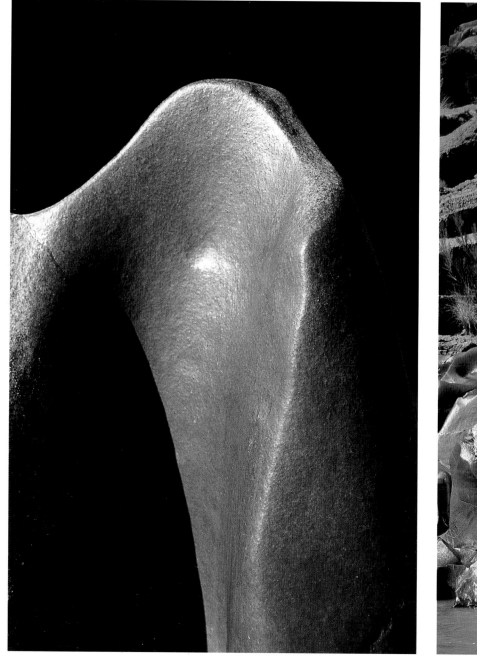

MILES 210-236

Chapter 9: The Lower Granite Gorge

The Diorite at Mile 212 (cont.)
Miles 211 and 212

opposite page left:
A single curve

opposite page right:
Sculpted diorite at river's edge, backed by rough limestone boulders

left:
Gleaming diorite

Little Bastard Rapid and Pumpkin Springs
Mile 212

above right:
Just below Little Bastard Rapid, sculpted Tapeats appears on the left, at Mile 212.6. One can easily walk back up to this area of shoreline from Pumpkin Springs, at Mile 212.8. In this photo, one sees both sculpted Tapeats and basalt.

Little Bastard Rapid and Pumpkin Springs (cont.)
Mile 212

opposite page:

With a backdrop of gleaming black rock, a kayaker surfs a perfectly formed wave in Little Bastard Rapid, at Mile 212.2.

above left:

Pumpkin Springs, at Mile 212.9

right:

A small arch in the Tapeats at Mile 212.6

MILES 210-236

217 Mile Rapid and The Lower Granite Gorge
Miles 215 to 217

opposite page:

The river stays in the Tapeats until Mile 215.1, where granite appears and the Lower Granite Gorge begins. Here, a motor rig runs 217 Mile Rapid at full throttle, guaranteeing a big splash. This rapid drops 16 feet and is rated 6-7.

Mile 220 Camp and Diamond Creek
Miles 220 to 225.6

above:

At Mile 220 camp, this is a telephoto view across the river of a hillside of Bright Angel Shale.

below right:

The large delta of 220 Mile Canyon hosts three lovely and spacious camps and is a good choice for the last camp before take-out at Diamond Creek. The canyon holds gardens of ocotillo and brittlebush, seen here in evening light.

**Mile 220 Camp and
Diamond Creek (cont.)**

Miles 220 to 225.6

left:

The uppermost of the three camps at Mile 220 is called Gorilla Camp because of the gorilla likeness of the rock promontory seen here silhouetted against the sunset sky.

above:

Evening primrose at Mile 222 camp

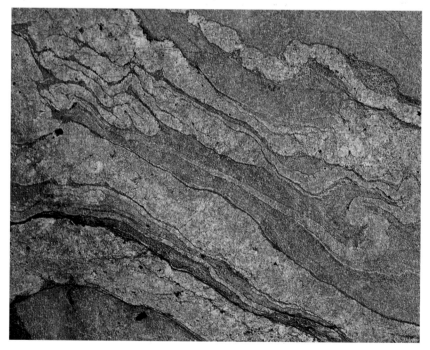

Mile 220 Camp and Diamond Creek (cont.)
Miles 220 to 225.6

above left:

At Mile 224.7, Diamond Peak stands at the entrance to a granite gorge that leads to Diamond Creek. Diamond Peak is named not for its profile but for quartz crystals found in the area.

above right:

Diamond Creek, at Mile 226, is the only side canyon in the Grand Canyon that provides road access to the river. It is the usual takeout for river trips (especially non-motorized trips) because of the presence of Lake Mead downstream. The takeouts on Lake Mead require trips to motor (or very seldom row—I've done it once) across a good expanse of lake. The Hualapai Indians, whose reservation incorporates this portion of the Canyon on river left, run their own commercial motorized trips from Diamond Creek to the lake. At trip's end, rafts dry out on the beach at Diamond Creek.

Below Diamond Creek
Miles 226 to 235.8

below right:

Gneiss, a metamorphic rock, seen at Gneiss Canyon, at Mile 235.8

opposite page left:

The waterfall and grotto of Travertine Canyon, at Mile 229

opposite page right:

A hole bored through a beachside schist boulder, near Mile 236. I end this photo journey here, in the vicinity of Lake Mead's farthest incursion upstream into the Grand Canyon, with a still free-flowing river.

Appendix:
The Major
Rock Formations
of the Grand Canyon

The geologic Law of Superposition states that "…in any sequence of sedimentary strata … that has not been overturned, the youngest stratum is at the top, and the oldest at the base; each bed is younger than the bed beneath, but older than the bed above it."

Kaibab Formation
270 million years old

Toroweap Formation
273 million years old

Coconino Sandstone
275 million years old

Hermit Formation
280 million years old

Supai Group
315-285 million years old

Redwall Limestone
340 million years old

Temple Butte Formation
385 million years old

Muav Limestone
505 million years old

Bright Angel Shale
515 million years old

Tapeats Sandstone
525 million years old

Grand Canyon Supergroup
1.2 billion - 740 million years old

Vishnu Basement Rocks
1.68 - 1.84 billion years old

350 feet (110 m)
250 feet (75 m)
300 feet (90 m)
300 feet (90 m)
1,000 feet (300 m)
500 feet (150 m)
0–50 feet (0–15 m)
450 feet (140 m)
350 feet (105 m)
0–200 feet (0–60 m)

HORIZONTAL SEDIMENTARY FORMATIONS
Kaibab Formation (a.k.a. Kaibab Limestone): 270 million years old, deposited in shallow seas
Toroweap Formation: 273 million years old, deposited in shallow seas
Coconino Sandstone: 275 million years old, petrified wind-blown sand dunes
Hermit Formation (a.k.a. Hermit Shale): 280 million years old, deposited in coastal swamps
Supai Group: 285-315 million years old, deposited in shoreline and near-shore environments
Redwall Limestone: 340 million years old, deposited in shallow seas
Temple Butte Formation (a.k.a. Temple Butte Limestone): 385 million years old, deposited in shallow seas
Muav Limestone: 505 million years old, deposited in shallow seas
Bright Angel Shale: 515 million years old, deposited in shallow seas
Tapeats Sandstone: 525 million years old, deposited in intertidal and shoreline environments

TILTED SEDIMENTARY FORMATIONS
Grand Canyon Supergroup: present only in a few locales and includes:
Dox Sandstone: 1090 million years old, marine deposit
Shinumo Quartzite: age undetermined, sand dunes
Hakatai Shale: age undetermined, marine deposit
Bass Limestone: 1250 million years old, marine deposit

METAMORPHIC AND IGNEOUS FORMATIONS
Schists and Gneisses: 1680-1840 million years old, metamorphosed sedimentary, igneous, and volcanic rocks
Granite and other igneous rocks: 1600-1700 million years old, igneous rock intruded into the Vishnu Schist

NOTE: Thicknesses vary in the canyon. Numbers are approximations for layers along the Bright Angel Trail in the central Corridor.

Photographing the Grand

All of the photos contained in this book were taken with 35mm cameras. For the last 15 years or so, I have used two Olympus OM-4 bodies, with a variety of lenses. The lenses are: Tokina 17mm, Tokina 28-70mm, Olympus 75-150mm, Olympus 85-200mm, and Olympus 50mm Macro. I particularly like the metering of the OM-4. Accessories I use are: polarizing filters, gradual split filter, power winder, OM T-32 flash, and a tripod. I use a tripod whenever possible while on shore, often climbing in canyons with one hand holding the camera mounted on the tripod, leaving my other hand free for climbing.

I started using Fuji Velvia 50 film when it first became available, pushing it one stop. Most recently, I have used Kodak E100VS and Velvia 100. I try to avoid faster films. And while on the subject of film, it's probably worth mentioning that the last trip of the series that led to this book, in the fall of 2003, came at a time when digital photography was really taking off. I purchased my first digital camera in 2004. Among other remarkable features of this camera, I can move at will (from shot to shot) between ISO 100, 200, and 400.

In photographing *The Grand,* I found that a full range of lenses was called for. Macro, of course, for the flowers. The "stacking" effect of telephoto lenses was used to advantage where there was a repetition of form (see photo on pages 118 and 119). Long lenses are, of course, needed to photograph distant objects, such as a raft in a rapid. Wide-angle and extreme wide-angle lenses were needed for capturing the whole scene when movement was limited (see photo of Redwall Cavern on page 38). Also, an extreme wide-angle lens used vertically provides that extra depth of field to maintain focus on very close foreground objects and out to infinity, simulating the effect one can get with the swings and tilts of a view camera (see photo of 75 Mile Creek on page 69). Shooting from a moving boat usually doesn't allow for the luxury of exchanging one fixed focal length lens for another. Zoom lenses are more practical for such fast-paced photography.

On my raft, I secure my waterproof camera box within an arm's length of my rowing position, so that I can get into it with the least delay. This makes a considerable difference in how many photos ultimately I can take. I can have my camera in my hand in a matter of seconds. Otherwise, it's my belief that established nature photographers are not necessarily more "talented" than you or me. In my opinion, the secret to success in this field is to be out there,

making yourself available to what nature has to show you. In the Grand Canyon, that means waking up very early, maybe letting your dinner get cold while you're taking pictures in the evening, taking pictures in the rain, never going anywhere without your camera and tripod, and so on. Throw in basic competency with your camera, of course. Then, when you're there for nature's great moments, you'll get great photos.

The Colorado River in the Grand Canyon is among the most worthy of locales in which to practice photography. There is something of interest or great beauty to be seen and captured every time you turn around. If you're a photographer, your Grand trip is an occasion to rise to. Take lots of film or a gigabyte or two of digital storage, your tripod, and an excess of battery power. And a back-up camera, just in case.

May the Canyon reward you with superlative photos—the very best way to remember the very best river trip in the world.

above:
Shutterbugs in action!

189

Acknowledgments

This book is the culmination of practically a lifetime of involvement in outdoor adventure and photography. Throughout this time, I have had the good fortune to make many friends who have been both companions and mentors. *The Grand* would likely not have come about without their influence and assistance.

First among these individuals is my best friend, David Hiser. We met as ski bums in Alta, Utah, in 1960. Years of skiing, mountaineering, and a shared passion for photography followed. David went on to a long career as a photographer for the National Geographic. Most recently, he has been teaching courses in digital photography. I got started on *The Grand* by attending a weeklong course on Photoshop taught by David, and he continued to provide indispensable assistance from that point on. His wife, Annaday, helped with the initial design of the book.

Another skiing and climbing companion from the '60s is Lito Tejada-Flores. He is a prolific author on many outdoor subjects, a reknowned ski instructor, a filmmaker, a publisher, and an expert in digital photography. He and his wife, Linde Waidhofer, an esteemed landscape photographer, team up to teach courses in digital landscape photography and digital lab techniques. They have both helped in the production of *The Grand* from beginning to end, and Lito wrote the Foreword for this book.

Again in the '60s, while attending the University of California, Berkeley, I took advantage of free photographic instruction provided by the staff of the Associated Students campus darkroom. They were top-notch, published photographers in the West Coast tradition of Ansel Adams and Edward Weston, and I doubt I could have found better instruction elsewhere. The staff included Dave Bohn and Roger Minick.

My son, Ethan, once a river guide with our family-owned New Wave Rafting Company, of Santa Fe, New Mexico, and self taught in Photoshop when it first appeared, is now a creative director. He has unfailingly helped to bring me up to speed on my Mac G4 and other matters both technical and aesthetic.

Molly McDow, also a former New Wave guide, got herself a masters degree in media arts and has provided invaluable advice at all stages of this project.

David Hiser, Peter Donahue, Linde Waidhofer, and my wife, Kathy Miller, contributed photos to this book.

Rob Elliott, the owner of Flagstaff-based Arizona Raft Adventures, which provides trips on the Colorado River in the Grand Canyon, has been a river mentor and reviewed the manuscript of this book.

Charles Abbott traded the use of his state-of-the-art Digital Arts Aspen workspace for river trips.

Getting a private (self-guided) Grand trip has never been easy. Thanks to Scott Vollstedt, Carol and Will MacHendrie, and Ted Turner for inviting Kathy and me on their private trips.

A make-or-break requirement for a successful multiweek Grand trip is companions who are both capable and easy to get along with. I have been fortunate to have had many such worthy companions. For the most part, they have been: guides and friends of New Wave Rafting Company; guides of Arizona Raft Adventures; my stepson, Brahm Reynolds, and my stepdaughter, Laina Reynolds-Levy, both also (you guessed it) former New Wave river guides; my son, Ethan; and, of course, my best river (and everywhere else) companion, my wife, Kathy. She appears often in these pages, and I hope that she is as easy on your eyes as she is on mine.

Both my parents always lovingly supported my predilections. My mom, 98 years of age at the time of this writing, is thrilled that I have finally amounted to something with this, my first book of photography.

Lastly, the crude prototype book I handed over to Wilderness Press was transformed into the artful book you now hold in your hands by the capable efforts of my editor, Eva Dienel, and designer, Jeremy Stout. We collaborated over many months, and their contributions are much appreciated.

Index